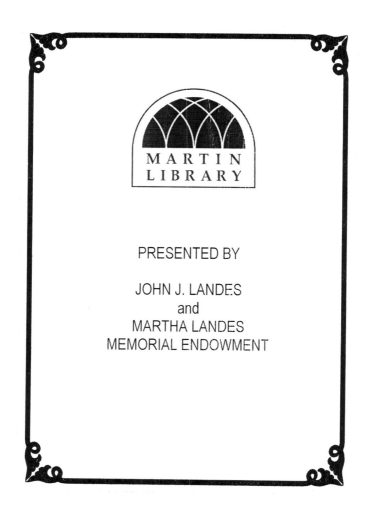

Influential Country Styles

Judith Miller
Influential
Country Styles

Photography by Simon Upton

Watson-Guptill Publications / New York

First published in the United States in 2006 by
Watson-Guptill Publications,
a division of VNU Business Media, Inc.,
770 Broadway, New York, New York 10003
www.watsonguptill.com

Conceived and produced by Jacqui Small LLP,
an imprint of Aurum Press Limited
25 Bedford Avenue London WC1B 3AT

Publisher Jacqui Small
Editorial Manager Kate John
Designer Maggie Town
Editor Sian Parkhouse
Contributing Writer Jill Bace
Production Peter Colley

Library of Congress CIP data is available from the
Library of Congress.

ISBN-10:0-8230-0954-8
ISBN-13: 978-0-8230-0954-1

Manufactured in Singapore

1 2 3 4 5 6 7 / 09 08 07 06

contents

influences

The universal appeal of the country owes
much to its unique role as an effective escape
from the pressures of urban life, for it is in
the universal vision of the simple pleasures
afforded by the countryside that one seeks
comfort, to relax, to be spontaneous, and
to live a natural, unselfconscious existence.

the rural idyll

ABOVE The prospect of gently dozing by an open fire
surrounded by exposed 18th-century brick in a favorite
comfortable armchair is all part of the joy of a lazy
weekend in the country for man—and his best friend.

OPPOSITE The gentle rippling of the Macedonia stream,
birds resting on the post and beam structure of the oldest
cider mill in Connecticut, built circa 1735, the first signs
of spring on the budding trees heralding warmer days
ahead—all part of the promise of country living.

Mention the word "country" and a host of colorful and familiar images spring to mind. Bouquets of dried herbs hung from rough-hewn ceiling beams perfuming the air of a rustic kitchen, an old walnut table gleaming with a timeworn patina, the faded fabric of a patchwork quilt casually tossed over a favorite rocking chair, a mismatched collection of vibrant hand-painted dishes assembled on the mantelpiece of a wood-burning fireplace—the portrait of the country look is conjured up in the imagination by these and hundreds of similar ideals that reflect the rural tradition.

For centuries the countryside has exercised an enduring influence on the interior decoration of houses dotted across the globe. The timelessness of country style remains indebted to the imagination and resourcefulness of the rural poor, who generally did not possess the money to follow the whims of fashion. Furniture, textiles, metalwork, ceramic pots, and tiles were created with an eye to what was simple, durable, and lasting. In this way the bucolic tradition that remains widely celebrated today was born: elaborate swags and pelmets and heavy drapery have no place in the country house, whose complexion by its very nature is continuously developing.

One of the charms of country living lies in its lack of pretension. Whether starkly simple or comfortably cluttered, the distinctive features that define country style are the most obvious ones: the desire for comfort, a respect for craftsmanship, and the integrity of design, the link between form and function, an appreciation for that which is old, well-loved, and boasts an abiding history, and an individuality that has been created from the assemblage of a variety of personal elements. These could be decorative family heirlooms such as a brightly colored quilt sewn by a great aunt and

RIGHT Nestled at the foot of Mount Albert lies a mining ghost town. Miners discovered gold here on July 4, 1879. By 1880, 300 people had arrived. Similar structures provide a perfect country escape.

OPPOSITE, TOP FROM LEFT A wooden cabin built in 1925 hugs the land on this island in the Oslo fjord. Local stone has always been the natural choice for rural builders as there was always plenty at hand. Vernacular buildings blend effortlessly with their surroundings as the stone weathers and ages. Traditional earth roofs are home to mosses and grasses which as well as insulation act as camouflage, making a house part of its setting. CENTER FROM LEFT The design of a country home holds many clues to its location. A gambrel roof is typical of New England, but has been used in France since medieval times. Former mill workers' cottages sit just across the creek from their workplace. Its plain design—inside and out—is proof of its humble origins. This traditional Connecticut Colonial house built circa 1735 has a central chimney with two front parlors and a large kitchen in the rear. BOTTOM FROM LEFT In rural Normandy a country courtyard garden is almost a tamed part of the landscape. It has its own formality, thanks to carefully tended lawns and box hedges. A Provençal courtyard—complete with ancient well—provides a shady corner for an open-air lunch. In Morocco, inner courtyards filled with the branches of overhanging palms and scented flowers provide a cool oasis from the sun. Terraces provide distant glimpses of the Atlas Mountains.

passed through several generations, a sturdy oak table in a warm kitchen that has borne witness to countless family meals, and which has served as both a cutting board and a repository heaving with recently picked vegetables or fruit from the garden, or humble decorative objects picked up on family vacations—shells, handpainted ceramics, woven baskets—that are cherished for the countless memories that they evoke. The essence of the country is wrapped up in such modest—albeit meaningful—details. The melange both of the old and the new, the well-worn and well-loved, the sharp contrasts of color alongside the subtle harmonies of hues, the variety of textures—all work together to give country style its special character.

An aura of romance and nostalgia surrounds the country lifestyle, for within its modest framework of simplicity, warmth, and candor lies a yearning for the past and the desire to pursue a mode of living that might all too soon be consigned to the pages of history. At once both decorative and hard-wearing, country style champions the merits of craftsmanship. It owes its genesis to the need for making much of little by those who had little money, and so the country remains a powerful symbol in the modern world, celebrating a way of life that has always been underpinned not by glamour and excess, but by self sufficiency and a respect for what is utilitarian. In the country people created interiors that were by necessity generous and long-lasting, and these put forth an agreeable alternative to the unrelenting, formally structured urban styles that tended to be embraced by those eager to be recognized at the forefront of what is considered to be fashionable. Having evolved throughout the centuries, the style that looks to the country for inspiration proffers a kind of freedom because it need not be confined to a single period in time. The homes created by country dwellers tended to change with the passing of every generation—chairs, beds, tables, and armoires were embellished or cast off, and walls frequently were renewed by

a sparkling coat of fresh and colorful paint. The key to authentic country style can be found in its celebration of sincere, uncomplicated informality as well as a reverence for, and appreciation of, honest and straightforward design.

The roots of country style derive from nature and the land. Around the world the country way of life is celebrated in a variety of interpretations, from Britain to Brazil, in Spain and in the South of France, and from New York to California. The hues of the landscape, the climate, the quality of light, the natural materials at hand for building and decorating and the prevailing architectural enterprises ultimately inspire and define the rural character of a region. For example, a low-built stone villa nestled in the rolling hills of the Tuscan countryside will reflect the mellow, warm palette of the surrounding landscape—faded pink, reddish-brown terracotta, yellow ocher, and burnt sienna—while a dwelling in Spain boasting vibrant contrasting colors and striking geometric motifs pays homage to an exotic tradition that looks to North Africa and the Moors for inspiration. In Sweden, by contrast, the traditional farmhouse—a familiar feature of the isolated rural farming communities sprinkled throughout Scandinavia—has been shaped by the rigors of a bitterly cold climate coupled with an abundance of forests in the vicinity. As with the houses that were built by the pioneers in the early years in North America, wood has been used both inside and out, from the steeply pitched roofs to the simplicity of faded pine floors and with painted decoration in the bracing, chilly colors—pale blue, gray, crisp white, and pale yellow—that are so evocative of northern climates.

Across the globe and throughout the centuries, interpretations of the cozy, informal country style have ranged from the elegant and grand to the rustic and pastoral. Yet at the heart of country style—whether luxurious or humble—lay a heritage of simplicity, informality, and a natural approach to living, its timeless charms symbolizing what is considered to be the archetype of an ideal way of life. Houses in the country—an opulent Spanish retreat, a cluttered cottage in the English Cotswolds, a clapboard shack on the coast of Maine—have typically tended to hold out against unpredictable and fanciful fashion trends. Country furniture, for example, tends to be robust, long-lasting, and relatively simply decorated. Thus furnishings for a grand country house in England pay tribute to the lack of pretension indicative of rural tradition by mirroring in modest oak or fruitwoods the sophisticated styles of the city, which were initially constructed using highly prized wood such as

mahogany or walnut and upholstered with sumptuous textiles. Even in a grand country house, fabrics remain relatively simple or in homespun print or check patterns, and ornamental embellishments are modest at best. Yet simplicity does not necessarily suggest a lack of sophistication, elegance or grace, and the country style adopted by a grand country house from sun-baked southern Italy to the far reaches of the Scandinavian provinces boasts humble treasures alongside a healthy dose of *savoire-faire*.

Looking at the country style from a more rustic perspective, it tends to be defined by what is straightforward and unpretentious, that which celebrates the homespun delights of a bucolic life and brings about a sense of comfort, warmth, and wellbeing. Simple and uncluttered, rustic country style does not turn its back on the cozy and pleasurable at the expense of the joys of decoration, preferring instead to favor the one of a kind, the flawed, the unconventional over the mandates posed by conventional taste and the formality of period styles. Honoring the rural past and celebrating the time-honored traditions of craftsmanship, it looks back to what has gone before, finding beauty in the faded, blemished paint finish of wooden plank panelling or a cupboard door, rejoicing in the rough-hewn construction and rich patina of a beech ladderback chair with a rush seat, or delighting in an oak table top boasting scars that look back to a legion of family dinners enjoyed over generations. It is in the simplest of things that beauty and wellbeing are to be found. Practical and functional objects—plates, candlesticks, baskets, spoons—rather than pointless knickknacks, and simple, plain-colored textiles are enjoyed as decorative ornaments that lend vitality and life to a home. The distinctive charm and rustic flavor that can be found

in a country interior owe much to an imaginative mixing and adding, a mellowing-over-the-years kind of softness and beauty that makes a highly personal statement while also reaping both pleasure and satisfaction.

In the 21st century the sense of country has evolved in yet another interesting way. Many designers use the canvas of an ancient building as the setting for a minimalist tableau. Here the fashionable icons of 20th-century design—a cupboard by Charles and Ray Eames, a Wassily armchair by Marcel Breuer, a Le Corbusier *chaise longue*—seem to be perfectly placed in a stripped-back 18th-century fieldstone cottage. They are united by a lack of pretension and simplicity. "Less is more" need not only apply to a designer New York loft, it can be very appropriate to the 21st-century country retreat.

What those who embrace a life centered around the countryside have in common is the deep-rooted desire for comfort and security, with nature and traditional furnishing a welcome sanctuary from the hectic pace and anxieties that tend to wreak havoc on everyday life. The charm of the pastoral idyll that originated centuries ago remains in the 21st century at once seductive and reassuring, giving rise to a welcome and longed-for serenity.

materials

OPPOSITE The rustic interior of this lodge in Aspen, Colorado, is constructed with massive standing logs killed by forest fires in Montana. The coped logs have an infill of polymer chinking to allow for the wood's natural shrinkage. The logs are left untreated and can still settle and crack with a sound not unlike distant thunder. The main room has enormous structural log cross members in front of the wooden spiral staircase, with banisters of branches with the bark left on—another back-to-nature touch. An indoor swing hanging from the ceiling and mounted deer and buffalo heads on the walls complete the natural look.

BELOW The wooden bed in this Norwegian cabin is called a *himmelseng*, or heaven bed, because the sleeper is protected by the structure. In addition to being a heavenly place to sleep, it is practical; there are drawers underneath— a useful addition as the room is deliberately small to preserve heat in the bitterly cold winters, and the bed is so big it leaves little room for other furniture.

wood

For centuries, wood has been the material of choice for the building of houses, the decoration of interiors, and the construction of furniture. A hard, sturdy, and flexible material originating from the trunks and branches of trees, wood is available in most parts of the world, is easily worked, and with care and consideration is eternally renewable.

Around the globe, houses and furniture have always been made with the materials that were most readily available, essentially growing out of the surrounding landscape. From the abundant forests of Scandinavia to the rolling plains of the Midwest, trees of all varieties have been used to provide shelter as well as create the comfortable, nurturing environment called "home", and it is in the style of the country where the strength, the warmth, and the enduring beauty of wood is shown to best advantage.

Woods are divided into two main groups: the hardwoods, which are produced by broad-leaved trees including ash, beech, oak, elm, and chestnut, and the softwoods that are derived from conifers, such as cedar, pine, spruce and yew. Each species of timber has unique properties of stability, durability, color, texture, elasticity, and hardness, which play a key role in determining which type of wood is best suited for a particular purpose. For example, the strength and durability of oak have traditionally made it the ideal lumber for the construction of houses, while the color, close grain, and hardness of walnut and mahogany make them especially suited to furniture making.

CLOCKWISE FROM TOP LEFT This 19th-century Pennsylvania gristmill is typically log and plaster and was adapted by architect Richard Williams to suit the vernacular architecture. Architect Ron Mason used traditional Scandinavian cope methods to build this mountain lodge in Colorado. This early 20th-century Norwegian log cabin was moved by boat from northwestern Norway to its present location on the Oslo fjord. The design of this typical Colonial house in Litchfield, Connecticut, was based on English George II style—the frame is post and beam faced with clapboard. The double-overhang indicates an early date, a holdover from Elizabethan building structures. Medieval builders used local wood to build the framework of this half-timbered house and then filled the gaps with wattle and daub. Wooden homes give and take from the landscape. The roof of this Norwegian cabin is edged with silver birch bark; the roof is covered with grasses and lichen. Coped logs treated with tar offer protection from the harsh climate.

Since the Middle Ages, the oak has taken pride of place as one of the timbers most widely used for furniture and building. English oak—of which there are more than 300 varieties—is generally considered to be the finest in quality, boasting as it does a rich, pale brown color and a texture that grows even harder and darker with age. Oak from the Baltic states, which is considerably softer and has a grain that tends to be much straighter than that found on most English oak varieties, was so favored for siding and paneling that it eventually became known as wainscot oak.

The craft of woodworking ranks among the earliest skills developed by man, and the natural properties of wood provide ample opportunity for the craftsman to demonstrate his talents. Wood lends itself naturally to a variety of techniques for furniture and interior decoration, including painting, carving and graining, veneering, gilding and lacquering. The country house—be it rustic or grand—tends to favor by its very nature the simplest and most straightforward decorative treatments. In the American colonial interior, wall paneling and furniture were frequently painted in deep earth tones—terracotta, blue, brick red, and moss green—while the Gustavian country style of Scandinavia embraced the cool, crisp colors reflected in the surrounding terrain, including shades of icy white and cream, pale pink, soft gray, and sky blue. Paint was traditionally applied to furniture and architectural woodwork to carry light and color into the heart of the house, as well to disguise any flaws that might be present in the grain and to camouflage lumber of inferior quality. Its appeal is enhanced by the fact that over time painted wood gains a careworn patina, adding a note of eccentric charm and a sense of the rural past to the interior of a country dwelling.

Other woodworking techniques that are particularly at home in the pastoral style include carving—of wall panels, over doors, and in the form of furniture crests and railings—and the practice known as graining, whereby furniture and architectural woodwork made from cheap softwoods such as pine are painted to simulate more exotic and expensive hardwoods.

In England, sumptuous Elizabethan and Jacobean interiors celebrated the beauty and majesty of oak by lining rooms with the pale, honey-colored wood arranged in square or rectangular panels, which were occasionally carved with a variety of motifs, including the well-loved linenfold that was designed to mirror the softly draped folds of linen cloth. This fashion for covering the walls of rooms with paneling of wood was taken up by the poor who were living more modestly throughout the countryside, although rarely did their efforts display the vigorous, high-quality carving that typically embellished the paneling decorating the more prosperous English country house. The comfort and warmth afforded by walls that have been enriched with wood paneling in oak, pine, or chestnut—to name but a few popular timbers—are also echoed in the tradition of covering floors with rough-hewn or highly polished wooden planks.

From England to continental Europe and across the Atlantic to colonial America, the dependence on wood for building houses or constructing furniture and interiors was ultimately dictated by the ready availability from enormous reserves of this cherished natural resource. A thatch-roofed cottage nestled in the English countryside shares with the traditional Scandinavian farmhouse and the lodges and cabins of the pioneering New Englanders and Pennsylvania Dutch in timber-rich America a dependence upon native woods to make pitched or gabled roofs, window frames, blinds and shutters, ceiling beams, floorboards, tables, chairs, and wall paneling. In a country house the interior depends upon its very architecture to put forth a decorative statement. The wooden planks that have been assembled to

CLOCKWISE FROM TOP LEFT Pickled and weathered finishes provide interesting contrasts in the hallway of this Belgian cottage. The structural beams are exposed; traditionally they would have been covered.
In contrast to the dark wood exterior, traditional country furniture, painted to match the rest of the décor, fills a simple modern Norwegian kitchen.
A reclaimed wood table and painted commode sit on a wooden floor in a South of France dining room. Although a relatively new build, features of the design, including the beamed ceiling, echo the style of the region.

Tongue-and-groove paneling made from southern yellow pine creates a comforting cocoon and blends well with a molded plywood Eames screen in a Colorado cabin.
A 1930s' bedroom set—complete with Bakelite handles—mixes with other 20th-century memorabilia in this upper New York state bedroom. The exposed ceiling beams show the ghosting of the original lathes.
The exposed wooden A-frame beamed structure is softened by the "medieval" seagrass floor covering and cool beige linens in this 18th-century English cottage bedroom.

BELOW The working area and maple cabinets in the kitchen of this Colorado cabin blend with the wood of the walls, floor, and ceiling, creating a homogenous interior. The kitchen is flooded with light from the glass doors and windows by day, and recessed spots and a Castiglioni Arco floor lamp by night.

BELOW Wooden beams are not always structural. Faux chinked walls combined with a wooden table, drawings by Kenyan artist Tonio Trzebinski, and red and white sheepskin rugs create an unusual yet warm and welcoming African and Alpine mix in the living room of this New Mexico mountain home.

create the structure of a house might also inform the interior surfaces of the rooms. From Stockholm to the Adirondacks, Madrid to Memphis, Provence to Santa Fe, there is a rich abundance of features such as a rough-hewn beamed ceiling, wall paneling shrouded in a warm honeyed patina, a well-defined, sharply carved balustrade, a cleanly lined window frame, a lavishly carved overdoor, or a wooden door that reflects the colors of the landscape—architectural elements such as these at once serve to decorate a room and work together to create a harmonious, commodious interior.

The unique qualities of wood make it the ideal material for building and furnishing a home in the country style. Although it can be vulnerable to damage caused by wood-boring insects, it is in its very strength and durability that the reverence for the rural past and its craftsmanship—so central to the idea of the country way of life—can be found. Both inside and out, with the passage of time wood takes on a rich, timeworn sheen. On the exterior of a Dorset farmhouse window shutters fade and weather, pitched roofs adopt a living green patina and are bleached by the sun, while a New England clapboard cottage shades to a charming silvery gray with repeated exposure to the seasonal vagaries of the elements. Inside the natural colors of wooden wall paneling, door frames, or floor planks continue to deepen over time or acquire a mellow glow, which helps convey the sense of inevitable aging, honestly presented, that is a cornerstone of country style.

With constant use—a scratched and dented table of scrubbed pine that has been at the center of countless family meals, a venerable oak sideboard, a scarred and knocked elm comb-back rocking chair that has been handed down from father to daughter, the aged, unadorned, oak floorboards that have born the weight of countless footsteps—wood comfortably pays tribute to all that has gone before, gradually absorbing and celebrating the imperfections that have been acquired with the passage of time.

Furniture made of wood—beds, tables, chairs, cupboards—is especially compatible to the rural interior, highlighting the warmth, the comfort, and the cozy lived-in feelings that are the long-established hallmarks of the rural lifestyle. The character of a country house tends to evolve over time, and furniture accumulated through a period of years—whether passed down through generations or acquired at random—will often span the centuries and embrace a host of historic styles. While some of the most simple types of wood furnishings tend to be traditionally linked with the homespun pastoral feel of the countryside—the oak kitchen hutch, the rush-seated ladderback chair produced by local craftsmen—many pieces decorating rural interiors were in fact provincial adaptations, rendered in local woods such as oak, elm, pine, birch, or fruitwoods, or the more luxurious mahogany,

cherrywood, and walnut furniture found in the most fashionable city dwellings. Other imaginative archetypes that have taken their place in the pantheon of country furniture made of wood include the rough-hewn rustic furniture made by local craftsmen in the Adirondacks that utilizes and celebrates the natural forms and irregular shapes of the raw material to form the end product.

The ambience and unpretentious character of an authentic country house interior are determined by a respect for the traditions and craftsmanship of the rural past, a delight in what is decorative and pleasing to the eye, and a celebration of the imperfections and charms inherent in what is both practical and functional. For centuries the countryside has produced architectural woodwork and furniture which, ripened with age, has been the material that brings comfort and creates a nurturing environment. From the Middle Ages to the Elizabethan era, from the 17th and 18th centuries, and onward to the Arts and Crafts movement and into the 21st century—the rich colors and distinctive grains and figure, the practical and hardwearing properties, along with the variety and versatility of wood—have defined and given voice to the country house aesthetic that continues to appeal and endure.

as nature intended

With great imagination and vision, two architects have created a sprawling assemblage of dwellings made of beautiful wood, nestled in the mountains of Colorado; an idyllic retreat that celebrates the majesty of its natural surroundings, their unusually arranged settlement represents comfortable living with a contemporary interpretation of the country-house style.

ABOVE The inspiration for Ron Mason's settlement comes from the mighty Arkansas River, famous for its rapids and whirlpools, and the surrounding native forests. While the original cabins hugged the land, the two most recent buildings are cantilevered over the river—making it an important focus of the design.

BELOW In 1990, Ron built the small log cabin guesthouse using the traditional Scandinavian "'coping" method of construction. He designed the large windows in the gable roof to allow his guests glimpses of the awe-inspiring local terrain and to bring the outside in.

There is hardly a better example to be found which proves wood to be the ideal material for building a country dwelling than the magnificent settlement created by architects Ron and Gillian Mason at Georgia Bar near Granite, Colorado. Bordered by the north end of the Collegiate Mountains—the peaks of Mount Harvard and Mount Oxford reach 14,000ft (4,300m)—the area takes its name from the barrier that runs along the edge of the Arkansas River, which was an important center of gold prospecting for migrants from Georgia from 1878 onward. Ron's passion for rivers and the sport of kayaking led him to this site during the 1960s, and in 1973 his dream of owning property on the river was finally realized when he bought the ranch from a woman with an out-of-date mining claim, living first in a tent and then in a Sioux-style teepee. Against the backdrop of dramatic rock formations, Douglas fir, spruce,

lodge pole and ponderosa pine, narrow-leaf cottonwood, and blue spur are among the indigenous flora that makes up the beauty of the surrounding landscape and underscore the settlement's close affinity with nature.

The settlement shares a deep-rooted connection with its natural surroundings, and since the buildings are not inter-connected, it has the feel of a small college campus or country village. It was a full decade after the purchase of the land before the first lodge of the settlement was finally built, constructed from the straight-growing logs found in a standing dead forest in the state of Montana. Believing there to be a genuine feeling of romance surrounding log buildings, Ron spent time in Finland learning about the cope method of construction that is popular in Scandinavia—where logs are cut and shaped into each other. The original lodge—measuring a sizable 18 by 48ft (5.5 by 14.5m) with a pitched roof constructed of galvanized steel and aluminum—boasts a living room, kitchen, bathroom, bedroom, and studio loft in pale golden pine. Sunlight from the surrounding landscape is brought into the interior with its gabled ceilings by expansive walls made of window glass that furnish breathtaking panoramic vistas of the mountains in the distance. By 1990 a small log cabin had also been erected nearby for use as a house for visiting guests. Once Ron had finally got the building of log cabins out of his system, he turned to a more modern aesthetic. The dining room—a highly original

OPPOSITE The main living room of the log cabin, built in 1983, is spacious and airy. All the logs are southern yellow pine. The house is used as a base for kayaking and walking in the summer and skiing in the winter, and hence the interior is kept simple. Faded native textiles enhance the mood.

cantilevered wooden structure suspended on stilts made of concrete and steel—nestles in a steep part of the embankment that is brimming with large loose boulders, and the difficult excavation of the site had to be done by hand using traditional methods. The lodge is virtually of the land.

To give the composition of the settlement a special focus, the most ambitious project of all—the building of a tower—soon followed, with Ron and Gillian doing their research by spending summers in Italy measuring towers that were central to villages of the Tuscan countryside. Rising to some 50ft (15m), the resulting tower—constructed of light-gauge steel and covered with southern yellow pine planks, which have been judiciously spaced to allow air and light to pass through unimpeded—plays host to a welcome army of hawks and eagles.

At night the tower is literally transformed into a glowing lantern, with light trickling through the siding boards, lending an atmospheric focal point to the heart of the settlement. Alongside the tower stands a small studio—some 12 by 36ft (3.7 by 11m)—with tongue-and-groove paneling made of honey-colored yellow pine, a radiant floor made of slate from Vermont, and a pitched roof bringing light in through windows placed across the gables. The elemental shapes of these structures boast a simplicity and timelessness that transcends connection with more fleeting trends in modern architecture.

ABOVE The dining room is a simple box, which appears to be suspended in a perilous position over the river. Diners enter confident that the concrete stilts it is built on are firmly anchored in the rocks. Everything about each of the structures has been designed with the spectacular location very much in mind.

ABOVE LEFT The dining room cube shows a more modern aesthetic than the other structures. It is constructed using shiplap joints and—with the exception of the floors—is left raw. Pendant lights set just above head height light the plain table and chairs, enabling diners to enjoy a meal in comfort without distracting them from the views.

LEFT The dining room is heated by a wood-burning stove, which provides a focal point for the room. Windows on both sides open to reveal the view and let in plenty of mountain air.

ABOVE The most recent structure, "The Tube," is cantilevered above the river and surrounded by indigenous trees including Douglas fir, Ponderosa pine, lodge pole pine, narrow leaf cotton-wood, and blue spruce.

RIGHT AND BELOW The Tube acts as a telescope to the Arkansas River. The orange window frame is filled with a pool of white light in winter when the river freezes. The view can be enjoyed from the comfort of an Alvar Aalto chair or while perched on a Japanese-designed stool. There is no need for art on these walls—the river and the landscape provide an ever-changing panorama; from local wildlife to enthusiastic kayakers testing their mettle on this complex river.

The most imaginative building in the settlement is also the most recent. Known as "The Tube," the box-car shape that resembles a treehouse is of a cantilever construction which has been located as close to the river as feasible, and anchored with a foundation made of poured concrete rather than one that has been built into the riverbank. It is the pure expression of an extraordinary vision, paying tribute both to raw Mother Nature and modern materials and building techniques. The entire space has been designed as a telescope to create a frame for the Arkansas River and the enveloping landscape. The aluminum window-frame walls are covered with powder-coated, scratch resistant orange paint that marries well with rusted steel. This vast picture window affords a constant distraction by offering a changing landscape before your eyes, as though captured through a telescope. Nothing else can distract the eye, which is irresistably drawn through to the wilderness beyond.

Carefully chosen to complement woods such as the maple used for the kitchen cupboards and a simple backdrop comprised of yellow pine paneling for walls, floors, and ceilings, the collection of furniture is a decorative amalgam of slick modern simplicity, from chairs designed by Alvar Aalto, and a screen and sofa created by Charles Eames to a lamp by Castiglioni.

a hillside retreat

In a quiet and picturesque setting overlooking the Rappahannock River and surrounded by tall trees stands a charming log cabin that is the essence of American country-house style. Originally built in Pennsylvania, the house was moved to a cattle farm nestled in the foothills of Virginia's majestic Blue Ridge Mountains.

ABOVE RIGHT The cabin overlooking the Rappahannock River in Virginia fulfills all the criteria of the romance and escape of the country idyll. The cabin at the edge of the woods nestles in splendid isolation on the tree-lined riverbank.

OPPOSITE AND RIGHT The front veranda overlooks the creek. Weathered rocking chairs and simple wooden stools blend with the log and plaster cabin walls, which have been chinked with Portland cement. This is a peaceful place to while away the hours watching the river flow by or waiting for dusk to fall before the lamps are lit.

Transporting buildings from one spot to another is a long-held tradition continued in the U.S., where great emphasis is laid on reuse—ours is not the purely disposable society dismissed by contemporary cynics. Buildings have always been deemed as precious, and it is very important to preserve a historical building in particular. Therefore it is not uncommon for some to be dismantled beam by beam, brick by brick and moved to another, more preferred, site, in this case, rural Virginia.

Part of the region known as Appalachia, the Blue Ridge Mountains boast a rich cultural heritage, from the traditional folk arts of poetry and storytelling to the unique sound of bluegrass music with its earliest roots in Civil War Appalachia. With a nod to the idea that buildings evolve over time—which is central to the country philosophy—architect Richard Williams of Solis Betancourt studied the vernacular architecture of the region surrounding the farm before adding a stone-sided extension to the original cabin "that works its way down the hill." Although built primarily of wood, the house has been built on top of stone foundations. Together the wood and stone forge a strong connection with the earth and a sense of continuity and permanence that lies at the heart of country style. So while the house has been recently renewed and restructured, it nonetheless exudes an ageless, timeless quality.

The extensive use of wood both inside and out lends the house a sense of homey comfort and coziness that adds to its charm. The outside verandah—with wood plank floorboards, a beamed ceiling, rustic tables, chairs, and stools and faced with siding made of rough-hewn logs and Portland stone—conjures up the image of a homespun pioneer dwelling. Various rooms of the house look out upon a stepped garden of natural quarried stone with box hedges surrounding a feast of colorful flowers and plants, including tulips, daffodils, forget-me-nots, snowdrops, and narcissi.

The warm and inviting interior has been lovingly assembled and reflects great attention to the smallest detail. For example, the walls have been plastered with the same Portland cement that was used for the chinking between the logs of the original 19th-century cabin from Pennsylvania; the ceiling beams were originally

BELOW Reclaimed wood has been used for the kitchen cupboards. Waxed to a golden brown, the wood still shows the hard-won signs of wear and tear from its previous incarnations. Traditional iron butterfly hinges and handles have been used to complete the aged look.

RIGHT Rustic kitchen utensils hang from a wrought iron bar by the stove. A bark basket is among the items sitting on the chestnut beam above.

OPPOSITE The welcome warmth of the kitchen and its association with friends, family, and shared mealtimes is an important part of the country ideal. Here loved ones gather around a 17th-century English oak refectory table, which is accompanied by a set of antique Windsor chairs.

part of a 19th-century Pennsylvania grist mill; the floorboards and window frames are of antique chestnut; and even the light switches are made of wood. Old barn doors made of chestnut also have been incorporated into built-in storage and closets. Throughout the house various types of wood have been used side by side to great effect, as in the master bedroom located in the stone-sided addition, where a faded antique pine fire surround complements the dark brown color of the chestnut floorboards. The house has been furnished in a style in keeping with the architectural framework, from a massive 17th-century English oak poster bed to a mahogany tripod table and walnut bachelor chest from the 18th century.

The combined kitchen/dining room at the heart of the house evokes powerful associations of home and hearth that are the hallmarks of the country lifestyle. Along with a large fire surround built of natural fieldstone, the walls and ceilings—which have been constructed from pale wood split beams and Portland stone infill—combine with the rich patina of the chestnut floorboards and the reclaimed cupboards in various shades of mellow wood to create a hospitable and comfortable atmosphere. The 17th-century English oak long refectory table and the Windsor chairs arranged around it are further reflections of the rustic simplicity and charm of country style.

cosmopolitan chalet

The country getaway for interior designer Alexandra Champalimaud and her family is a delightful hideaway above the town of Taos located in the north-central part of the state of New Mexico. As you climb into the mountains, the awesome beauty of the snow-capped peaks and dense forests is a constant reminder of the wildness of this retreat.

ABOVE Nestling beyond the slopes of the Taos Ski Valley in New Mexico, this cabin shows a modern take on the rustic look.

RIGHT In the kitchen the faux chinked walls provide a traditional foil to the almost space age gleam of the brushed steel appliances, the suspended table, and the spider-legged stools. Minimal spotlights hang from the plank ceiling.

and undeniable connection to the land, creating a modern refuge not unlike the teepees of the Plains tribes or the original log cabins built by the earliest pioneers.

But the kitchen and bathroom speak to another aesthetic, as the country-style wooden planks and floorboards that have mellowed over time and look back to the pioneer tradition—coupled with marble and wrought iron—serve as a showcase for slick, shiny modern materials such as brushed steel and glass, which have been used for high-tech appliances including ovens and sinks, as well as for tables and chairs. For this cabin manages to combine functionalism and a delightful feel.

ABOVE RIGHT Simple linen curtains hang from wrought-iron poles at the windows. The neutral color of the fabric contrasts with the wood and its stripes of interfill and the soft suede used to cover a 17th-century wooden-framed Italian armchair.

BELOW RIGHT The horizontal lines of the faux chinked walls are broken up by prints of Native Americans set in simple wooden frames.

Situated near Taos Pueblo—the Native American village and tribe from which it takes its name – the wooden cabin provides a comfortable escape from the rigors of the winters and the occasional black bears that idle over the road. The snow-capped mountains and pine forests of the Taos ski valley form a picturesque backdrop. Established following the Spanish conquest of the Pueblo villages, Taos—the name means "red willow" in the Tiwa language—became home to a budding art colony during the later part of 19th century. This artistic connection is still very much evident in the small town below, but also as you enter the Champalimaud cabin.

Nestled in this very romantic setting, the house has been constructed of wood with a peaked roof in the traditional style of a simple country chalet. It is the interior decoration, however, that captures the imagination and truly illustrates how very modern the style of the countryside can really be. The rich, warm patina of the wooden floorboards, rough-hewn ceiling beams, and chinked plank-wood wall paneling, ranging from pale honey and faded straw tones to shades of golden red and almost-black, reflect the variegated colors found in the surrounding countryside and successfully serve to bring a feeling of the the outside in. This highly original and inspired combination of colors and textures gives every room a strong

ABOVE A brushed steel sink set in a marble tabletop brings contemporary style to the bathroom, while the wooden walls and floors provide warmth and a feeling of age.

Against a backdrop of mostly pale, neutral shades for linen curtains, bedcovers, and upholstery, an exotic flavor threads through each room of the house. A variety of cultures is represented, ranging from the African to the Alpine, the local Native American to 17th-century Italy and the India of the Raj: these unlikely companions all mix happily together. Distinctive touches are evident everywhere, such as animal skins or woven rugs in shades of warm reds and pinks scattered across the wooden floors and on the over-stuffed, comfortable sofas, old as well as new pictures depicting Native Americans alongside drawings by a contemporary Kenyan artist, a simple wooden Spanish chest, a lavishly appointed Rajhastani bed highlighted by cone-shaped Indian lanterns, a table of dhou wood containing elephant bones—the origins of these richly diverse, highly decorative, and, not forgetting, always useful furnishings span the globe as well as the centuries.

The mix of old and new is seamless and never jars; the juxtaposition of items from different cultures is masterful. Everywhere the eye is entertained by the unexpected. And while the house and its colorful interior might not conform to the traditional concept of country style, it successfully sums up the mantra that lies at the heart of the country philosophy: everything belongs, no matter from what culture, century, or country. A country house is at its heart an eclectic magpie.

hewn out of the land

Perched atop Norway's isolated Hardangervidda—an extensive mountain plateau located in the southwestern part of the country that is the highest in Northern Europe and a drive of nearly four hours from Oslo—can be found a wonderfully cozy rural escape that brings special meaning to the country way of living.

ABOVE The outside walls of this Norwegian cabin are protected by a durable coat of tar. Here on the Hardangervidda, which is the highest mountain plain in Europe, the harsh terrain is speckled with an array of wildflowers, moss, and lichen.

RIGHT Pale woodwork and plenty of white china increase the amount of light in this corner of the kitchen. Crisscross molding on the drawer fronts add visual interest, as do the striped rugs on the floor. A set of 19th-century French storage jars sits on the wooden work surface.

In 1991 Mathilde Fasting and her husband—whose parents have owned an old cottage nearby since the 1950s—finally realized their longstanding dream of owning their own cabin in the area, which they have contrived to tie to the land with an imaginative marriage of local wood and fieldstone.

The indigenous communities that live in these areas are the most isolated in Europe, separated by high plains and even higher mountains and also the ferocity of the Arctic winters; the snow and severe frosts, howling winds, and interminable darkness. In this barren and rugged surrounding landscape, where even the local flora struggle to stay alive—the one-story dwelling lies very low, having been constructed using traditional methods that include digging down very deep into the rock to create the foundations and treating the coped logs on the exterior with tar to form a strong airtight bond that will protect against the harsh rigors of the weather. The gutters running round the roof are further protected by the use of a layer of silver birch. All these building methods are tried and tested to create a safe and weather-tight refuge. Local grasses sprout from the peaked roof of this rural hideaway, where rocks covered with lichen, a host of different wildflowers, ferns, clovers, mountain berries, and *reinlar*—a gray-white reindeer moss that grows surprisingly tall—mix happily together to create a breathtaking setting of stark natural beauty.

LEFT Windows ranged along the kitchen walls let plenty of light into the room and provide far-reaching views from the simple farmhouse table, known as a *langbord*. The table was originally much longer, but it has been shortened to fit the room. It is surrounded by a mixed set of 19th-and 20th-century pine chairs, all showing a homogenizing covering of distressed old paint.

RIGHT The colors of the paint and furnishings in the cabin are all taken from the stone and grasses around the cabin. The sofa and armchairs are covered with welcoming cushions and a vase of mountain flowers (*engsmelle*, or maidens tears) sits on the table. Simple white voile curtains hang at the windows. The cabin is called *Lykkg*, which means happiness in Norwegian.

BELOW A 19th-century painted chair and an old milk churn stand on the slate floor. The churn was purchased in a local antique store.

OPPOSITE A traditional covered bed and matching bunk beds were built for the guest bedroom. The dark wood contrasts with the airiness of the rest of the house. Knitted throws and simple gingham linen add a friendly, homespun touch.

The house relies upon the outside to inform the interior. Every color has been carefully chosen with an eye to nature and the color palette taken from the surrounding environment, with paint pigments for furniture, walls, and plank floors reflecting the pale cream, gray, silvery, mushroom, and yellow hues of the flowers, stones, and grasses found in the mountain landscape. Fabrics also link the outside to the inside, with the simple, almost-transparent curtains that furnish each room bringing in as much light as possible. The fabrics are mainly American—hinting to the link between these homes in the Old Country and the fabrics needed for the homes the immigrants built in New England. Fireplaces of local stone vie with an electric heating system buried beneath the floorboards keep the cabin cozy and warm to ward off the chilling winds that whip about.

The heart of the house—the kitchen—carries forth the theme of the countryside and embraces the pale color theme, as the cool, icy shades of the painted cupboards, ceiling, and wall paneling and floorboards are coupled with an antique pine farmhouse table—which was originally much longer and is known as a *langbord*—a mixed set of pine chairs from the 19th and 20th centuries boasting timeworn coats of old paint, and a scattering of rugs that were handmade by Mathilde. The serene and simple atmosphere that flows from the kitchen is only punctuated by a brightly patterned *fillerye* rag rug that proffers a cheerful shot of bright color.

Another delicious decorative touch can be found in the traditional Norwegian furniture dotted around the house, such as in the spare bedroom, where a practical built-in bed with drawers underneath—a *himmelseng*, or 'heaven bed', so-called because one is entirely covered—forms the centerpiece of the room. A painted corner cabinet, an early 18th-century *kannestol* dresser from Telemark, and a built-in box seat are coupled with some carefully considered details—an antique chair, an old butter churn, a painted wooden bucket filled with wildflowers—which all add to the country feel and rustic charm of this cabin located in the most remote mountains of Norway.

stone

Stone is a natural building material that has evolved over millennia through a series of geological processes and which can be found in various forms in all regions of the world. For thousands of years it has been used for the construction and ornamentation of buildings, as the base for inscriptions, for sculpture, and for decorative objects.

Rocks of stone are broadly defined by their composition of one or more minerals, by their texture and chemical composition, and by the means by which they have been created. The hardness, durability, color, and texture of stone varies widely, which has determined the ways in which it has been used, ranging from the sharply defined features of a portrait sculpture, the sumptuously carved detail on a decorative urn, the rough-hewn siding on the walls of a farmhouse, or the unevenly placed tiles of a sun-baked veranda. The sharp edges and undercut forms of a lavishly carved ancient Greek Corinthian capital, for example—while ideally suited to the even texture of marble and its ability to take and preserve fine detail—would be impossible to render from a hard, coarse-grained stone such as granite.

Up until the arrival of mechanized transportation, stone was traditionally procured from neighborhood quarries—from the rich marble deposits of Carrara in Italy to the strip mines of Colorado and the porphyry of Egypt—although exceptions inevitably ruled when there was a demand for a stone of a particular color or quality or where the locally available stone proved to be

OPPOSITE, CLOCKWISE FROM TOP LEFT
Stone can be treated in many ways in building; often it is rough-hewn, sometimes dressed, but local stone ties a house into the landscape. This classic Connecticut Federal house was built from local fieldstone in 1827. The locust trees, often called "lightning trees" locally, are a natural conduit for lightning strikes. Honeyed local stone was used to build farm cottages in this Cotswold valley in 1740. The building has gone through many transformations since it was built, including being a pub in the 1840s. It is now a gracious country house. The small windows with stone lintels are a local feature, as are the Gothic-inspired ground-floor windows.

Local stone was used to build this former farmhouse and cowshed in the late 19th century in Tarn et Garonne near Toulouse, France. Due to the intensity of the heat in the near desert a few miles from Marrakech, Morocco, the massive stone walls with small windows and doors surround shaded courtyards. The walls are built traditionally, with irregular stones, straw, and sand.

RIGHT This house was built on the site of an old orangerie in the hills above Cannes, France. It was built in 2001 using old local stones. This type of construction, which was used by the Romans, is known as Genoise.

unsatisfactory. Throughout history stone for building—either for economic reasons or due to a lack of technological expertise—was frequently acquired by reusing stone that had been previously worked. Employing stone in the construction of your home that had enjoyed another life was also viewed as an expression of wealth or of religious supremacy, as witnessed by the prestige enjoyed by early Islamic mosques for their use of columns that have been rendered in timeworn stone or by the ancient columns that were reused to build the west front of St. Mark's Basilica in Venice.

Stone has long been a salient feature of country architecture, both inside and out—from the cobbled streets and thick walls of the farmhouse, or *mas*, reflecting the intense, sunny colors of the rural Provençal landscape, to the arched doorway of a Spanish hacienda, to the rough-hewn hearth that brings warmth to a pioneer-style cabin located in the upper northern reaches of New York state. The walls of a low-built Tuscan villa that are made of stone have traditionally been covered with stucco in shades of pale pink or golden ocher, while flagstones pave the kitchen floor of an English country cottage, and the terrace of a Spanish courtyard is dressed in a stone chip pattern. Stone adds warmth and softness as well as an informal, rustic flavor to the country-house style, and it marries well with other materials, such as terracotta roof tiles or local timbers including walnut, chestnut, and oak that have been favored for architectural features—ceiling beams, door frames, and floor boards—and furniture—tables, chairs, cupboards, and bureaux.

The different types of building stone that have held sway for centuries across the globe for country architecture include limestone, marble, and sandstone. Limestone—an easily worked, soft, sedimentary stone made up largely of calcium carbonate and found in a wide range of colors and textures and particularly at home in Greece—welcomes fine detail and has been used from antiquity for building, architectural carving, and sculpture. The country-house interior has often benefitted from the use of limestone—for a carved fireplace surround, a robust kitchen sink, or flagstone floor tiles, for example—which bring into a room a soft, almost humble character. Travertine—a hard limestone ranging in color from creamy gray to yellow, brown, or red that was used extensively by the ancient Romans for building—remains a popular modern choice as a siding material.

Another building fabric that has often found its way into the country house—albeit on a grander scale and which is synonymous with the architecture of Italy—is marble. Composed primarily of calcium carbonate, marble is simple limestone transformed into something more luxurious by heat or pressure bearing down on the limestone. Pure calcium carbonate results in a white marble, although other components present in the limestone—such as iron or clay—will also be altered, thereby giving rise to the much-admired, diverse range of colored marbles. Marble can be found all over the world and throughout history has taken pride of place for building, architectural ornament, and sculpture. The beauty of the material,

known as York stone has been widely used as a building stone as well as cut into roof and floor tiles—in particular for the paving of both country-style kitchens and rustic garden terraces, as it is equally durable outside as indoors.

Over the centuries a variety of techniques have been used to transfer a building design from the architect to the craftsman working in stone. Carvers in ancient Rome and medieval Europe frequently worked by eye from rough sketches to bring to life complex, detailed ornament. This method was quicker and more flexible than taking measurements from a detailed drawing, which was the practice favored by architects in the Islamic world. From the late Middle Ages on, as paper became increasingly available, measured drawings became ever more common, and architects began to produce detailed specifications for all carved elements in a building.

Stone takes shape by the removal of excess material, and the method for doing this is determined by the character of the stone itself and the tools available. Hard stones, abrasives, chisels, drills, and saws have traditionally been used to create square-cut blocks for building as well as the elaborate flourishes of a lavishly carved fireplace surround. The carver would rough out the whole form before introducing detail and creating surface finish, an approach that avoids removing too much material too soon in the process.

Hard stones, such as marble, granite, and various dense limestones—for example, Purbeck marble quarried from the Isle of Purbeck off the Dorset coast in the south of England—can be polished to a high sheen by using progressively finer grades of abrasive. Sand, sandstone, emery, and diamond, when mixed with water as a lubricant, have been used as abrasives, which can be applied selectively to create variations in texture on the surface of the

the delicacy of detail that can be achieved through carving, and in particular the difficulty and expense of acquiring colored marbles—these are features that have typically implied status and wealth. In contrast with the informality that tends to be more characteristic of limestone, marble has traditionally enriched the more opulent country house, used for the glossy expanses of tiled floors, for lining the walls of a bathroom, as the sumptuously carved fireplace forming the striking centerpiece and focal point of a room or—taking inspiration from classical antiquity for something a little grander—even as a sensitively carved tabletop or decorative urn.

Last in the trio of sedimentary building stones that are found in most corners of the world—but which are especially at home in southern Italy, the island of Sicily, southern Spain, and the north of England—and which have played a key role in country-house architecture is sandstone. Comprised of grains of quartz mixed with sand, it appears in a broad range of colors—from white, yellow, red, and blue to brown and shades of pale gray—and has long been favored for building, tiling, paving, and carving. The pale, fine-grained sandstone originating in the southern part of Yorkshire in England

OPPOSITE ABOVE A converted 19th-century single-storey farm building in East Anglia, in which architect Anthony Hudson installed an internal knapped flint wall, a local material found within three kilometers of the barn.

OPPOSITE BELOW The owners of this Pennsylvania house, built by German settlers around 1800, wanted to enjoy the local fieldstone and use it as the inspiration for their decoration throughout the house. The interior allows a comfortable mix of old and new—19th-century French country chairs with an iconic Saarinen table from the 1950s.

RIGHT Rising up against a rustic stone wall, a simple modern staircase made from steel 'I'-profile beams has had wood trimmings added for the treads.

RIGHT In this wooden cabin in the Hardangervidda mountain plain in Norway, the main fireplace is built from local fieldstone, which still has lichen growing on it.

OPPOSITE This log lodge in Aspen, Colorado, has a fireplace constructed from local large rocks, also covered in lichen. Although showing influence from the camps of the Adirondacks, this lodge is undeniably Western with its huge scale, long vistas, and light. It is also reminiscent of the great lodge in Yellowstone National Park.

BELOW The Captain Daniel Lord house in Litchfield, Connecticut, was built in 1735. It is a typical early 18th-century Colonial house, which is bank built into the side of a slope so you enter on two levels—the wooden-sided main house is above ground and here in the stone foundations of the house you enter the summer kitchen. Cooking here meant the rest of the house did not get too warm. The French walnut armchair, the 18th-century English oak table, the English William and Mary-style cupboard, and the 16th-century German brass dishes are typical of the items wealthy immigrants would have brought with them to the New World.

finished work. Softer stones are worked smooth with a chisel or by dragging a blade across the surface. Worked stones are typically joined together with mortar, metal clamps, or ties or by means of molten lead, which has been poured into small canals that have been chiseled into the blocks.

The architecture of the country house seems to spring from the bosom of the earth, and it is perhaps in building materials such as the various types of stone—marble, granite, sandstone, limestone—that the humble, rustic character of the country is most widely appreciated and understood. Born of the surrounding terrain, country style—from a stone hunting lodge in the Périgord region of France, a whitewashed villa nestled in the American South that reflects the languid immigrant tradition of the Caribbean, or the rustic stonework detailing that is typical of an Arts and Crafts interior—it is in the mellow timeworn hues of the local landscape, a quiet, cozy, and comfortable mood, and a soft naturalness that speaks to the passage of time where the appeal of stone is most vividly realized.

timeless elegance

The house owned by Richard Ferretti and James Gager in northern Pennsylvania is a splendid testament to the enduring appeal and integrity of stone and the way that country-house style was dictated by the surrounding landscape. Dating from around 1800, it is built of the indigenous fieldstone from neighboring quarries that was commonly used by the early English and German settlers who found their way to the Bucks County area.

TOP LEFT Local fieldstone was the favored building material of the German and English settlers in northern Pennsylvania in the late 18th and early 19th centuries. This basic stone house, built in 1800, has a clapboard extension.

ABOVE James and Richard wanted to see the stone in every room. They stripped off the plaster and found that the hues in the local stone provided the color scheme. The sofas in this upstairs room are modern and comfortable—the colors, taken from the stone, are muted and subtle.

RIGHT To create such a simple, natural environment requires tremendous attention to detail. The floor is laid with Japanese blue slate, which reflects the color of the stone walls. This leads through to the kitchen; the modern white lacquered units were designed to maintain a linear uniformity, with a worktop of honed granite. Nothing should disturb the enjoyment of the natural surroundings—neon-tubing flush with the ceiling provides the lighting, the heating system is underfloor, and speakers for the sound system plastered in the wall.

In this historic and beautiful part of Pennsylvania, the house—boasting a clapboard extension—exudes an earthy, homegrown quality reminiscent of the Quaker simplicity that over several centuries determined architectural style. Pennsylvania and the nearby Delaware Valley long played host to an influx of European immigrants who brought with them a masonry tradition that looked back to the Roman Empire for inspiration. The Germans and Swiss in particular built solid fieldstone houses supporting steeply pitched roofs that reflected the medieval styles of northern Europe, and this trend eventually spread to other states, including North Carolina, Virginia, Kentucky, and Tennessee.

Although the interior had been decorated with an eye to the modern and the minimal, the extensive use of stone throughout demonstrates a healthy respect for the colonial country tradition and the rich history of its European ancestors. That stone plays such a prominent role in the architecture of the house—both inside and out—has much to do with the taste and sensitivity of the owners, who wished to forge a strong relationship with the past as well as with nature. Ever mindful of the architectural integrity of the house, they visited the nearby quarry to become familiar with the local Pennsylvania fieldstone, and made the decision that the primary decoration should depend upon stone.

ABOVE In the master bedroom the focal point is again the stone—the coursed random rubble with rough-faced stones laid like a jigsaw puzzle. The floors on the upper two stories are made from barn sidings.

With this idea in mind, the house was lovingly returned to its historic roots, by painstakingly stripping away layers of plaster and paint in every room they exposed the original splendor of the simple, uncluttered stonework. They wanted the house to exude a tranquil timeless quality—the stone itself has taken millions of years to form.

The house is grounded in its surroundings. Every aspect of the renovation of the house, down to the tiniest detail, was carefully considered. Everything in the house looks untouched, but everything has been changed. The intention to create a clean, natural environment witnesses various types of modern stone used throughout the house which set off the original aged structure of the rough-faced rubble stones laid like a jigsaw puzzle on the walls—for example, the Japanese blue slate covering the dining room floors and the honed granite surfaces of the kitchen. Stone plays the central decorative role in every part of the house, a unifying feature within the house, and one that inevitably links it to the surrounding landscape, bringing the outside in and tying it to an enduring sense of the past.

The interior of the house is furnished in a clean, simple, and primarily modern style—classic chairs by Charles Eames and Mies van der Rohe, neon lighting, paintings by a local artist. and a table by Eero Saarinen, for example—that complement its historic beginnings in the early 19th century. Colors—from ceiling beams to the fabrics covering sofas—tend to be muted, subtle. and unobtrusive so as to rest the eye and not detract from the architectural integrity of the house. But what is especially interesting is how stone has been employed not only as the architectural backdrop, but also how it accommodates in highly original ways and with great attention to detail the comfortable, modern interior—underfloor heating, for instance, or the speakers of a music system hidden inside the walls.

In keeping with the time-honored philosophy associated with country-house style, the natural materials that informed the surrounding landscape have also been applied to the exterior of the house. The contrived formality of the garden paving was replaced with locally quarried stone and planted with shrubs and trees to reflect and pay tribute to the surrounding landscape.

ABOVE Resting on the Japanese blue slate floor, the central pedestal dining table was designed by Eero Saarinen and the chairs by Charles and Ray Eames. The idea was not to find modern furniture, but the choice was dictated by the search for classics of shape and style. When James and Richard found the house, they felt it looked in on itself, so they inserted the wall of glass doors to bring the outside in.

LEFT The staircase was designed with an iron frame and brackets and massive slabs of unfinished walnut. The wooden stool was designed by Charlotte Perriand, and the chair was manufactured by Knoll in the 1940s. The simple white walls draw the focus back to the fieldstone— timeless, primal, and sensual.

a statement in stone

Nestled in the ravishingly beautiful landscape of Kent, Connecticut, the Federal stone house owned by the Keswin family, with interiors designed by Jeffrey Bilhuber, is the quintessential romantic ideal of country living—it is a building that at once indigenous to its place within the land and that honors its architectural integrity.

ABOVE This dramatic Federal stone house was built in 1827 in Kent, Connecticut, for a prosperous mill owner, Garret Winegar. It was designed as a grand status building very close to the road and overlooking the Berkshires.

Built in 1827, the house is situated very close to a main road—a feature common to grand status houses of the late 18th and early 19th centuries—and is surrounded by woods overlooking the picturesque Berkshire Mountains. This area of Kent was made rich by the fertile bottomland of the Housatonic River and the rich iron-ore of the mountains. It is important to notice the prominent position of this house—the owner wanted his house noticed. Most houses of this period were constructed of wood, and to build such an impressive and grand house in stone was like putting your bank balance on the walls!

There exists a strong synergy between the architecture and the interior. Stone forms not only the very foundation of this country dwelling, but plays a starring role for the decoration of the interior, lending a sense of stability and continuity that are hallmarks of country style and which are sorely lacking in modern prefabricated structures. Walls constructed from

different shapes and sizes of stone bring color as well as decorative pattern and texture to the architecture of every room in the house, from the chunky, rough-hewn pale fieldstone in the dining room to the broad, bold shapes in charcoal and sage that give the kitchen its special country character.

The color palette of the interior is subdued and atmospheric, derived from the somber hues of Connecticut fieldstone. To ignore the colors of this dominant structural element would be to fight against the very nature of the house itself. The pale muted shades of taupe, platinum, and gray marry well with sage, celado,n and robin's egg blue for cupboards, ceiling beams, wall paneling, and fire surrounds, to create a tranquil setting inside that also reaches out to the fragrant locust trees and flowers in the sumptuous gardens surrounding the house. The cool, clean palette is matched by strong touches of obsidian—a strong brown-based colour—that has been used to paint all woodwork,

LEFT AND OPPOSITE In the main dining room, the Connecticut fieldstone is left exposed on the outside wall. This was originally two rooms, and each end has a painted wooden paneled fireplace wall installed in 1928. Each has an English Regency convex mirror. The north–south design of the room is further emphasized by two identical contemporary Swedish tables surrounded by English Regency mahogany dining chairs and contemporary leather-covered chairs. The palette has been chosen by Jeffrey Bilhuber to subtly enhance the natural hues of the stone. Bright colors would have fought it, white would have killed it; instead he went for taupes, platinum, and grays.

including doors, built-in closets, and window shutters and frames. This is in keeping with the 18th-century practice—with fires typically roaring on the hearth throughout the day and into the night, the walls were dry brushed to keep them clean and a dark color is more practical.

In general, the furnishings scattered about the house remain simple, a concept that emphasizes the comfortable atmosphere. Mismatched chairs and tables painted in muted colors, fabrics in crewelwork, and the odd basket or pottery bowl randomly placed to add a spare, decorative touch highlight the simplicity and integrity that are hallmarks of country-house style.

ABOVE As you enter the main hallway, the palette is brighter, while still reflecting the lighter colors in the stone walls. The late 18th-century American mahogany table with finely tapered legs seems almost *en pointe*.

RIGHT Exposing the natural stone in an upstairs bedroom also shows the wooden elements of the early 19th-century construction. Modern wood beams painted in pale taupe further strengthen the structure. The darker taupe painted cupboards and the pale gray shutters have an almost Shaker-like simplicity, as has the 19th-century painted metal chair.

OPPOSITE The internal stone walls in the breakfast room are relieved by a window into the kitchen and are banded by two wooden beams, all painted in obsidian—a brown-based gray. In the late 18th to early 19th century, millwork (the crown molding, baseboards, and so on) was painted in dark colors for practical reasons. The 19th-century cupboard has wonderful original paint.

French farmhouse

Nestling at the foot of the Pyrenees, the city of Toulouse—known as "la Ville Rose" because of the delicate purplish-pink hues of its charming buildings—boasts a rich past. Once a major metropolis, it sank into sleepy regional-level status in the 18th century, missing the Industrial Revolution. This helped to protect its distinctive architecture.

ABOVE RIGHT A typical stone farmhouse and barn for Blonde d'Aquitaine cows, near Toulouse in Tarn et Garonne, was built in the 1870s and was recently redesigned by Kathryn Ireland. The structure is traditional in that it has courses of rough stone with brick courses around the shuttered windows.

OPPOSITE The evening summer dining room in the old cowshed was quite deliberately left very natural and untouched—apart from the addition of large, old terracotta tiles on the mud floor. This is the essence of southern French country living— the simple table that can be extended to accommodate extra guests, painted country chairs, brightly colored fabric, metal chandeliers that can be lowered on ropes, and jugs of local wine and plentiful plates of delicious food from the village market.

RIGHT In the same room, implements left over from the working farm have been left where they always were. Instigating change for change's sake has been strongly resisted.

Not far from this bustling and newly regenerated city on the banks of the Garonne River and the Canal du Midi, with its pretty squares and grand boulevards, luxuriant parks, historic churches, and magnificent townhouses with shaded gardens, can be found the equally picturesque village of Tounis. Here, amid the beautiful rolling hills, fabric and interior designer Kathryn Ireland has created a delightful country retreat where nature plays an important role both outside and in her home, and the surrounding environment has played an integral role in her work, by helping to inspire some of her fabric designs.

Surrounded by a garden filled with lemon trees and blackberry bushes, old English roses, and hydrangeas, the old stone farmhouse dates to 1870 and boasts a barn that was originally used to house the local variety of Blonde d'Aquitaine cows. A typical vernacular building that has evolved from a two-room farmhouse with extensions added over the decades, it owes its dazzling and seductive charm to its unplanned and organic character. What remains particularly striking is what the owner has *not* imposed upon the original structure to make this a comfortable and modern refuge. It has been left to evolve and breathe, its imperfections, natural surfaces, and textures celebrated and the surrounding landscape a powerful and lasting influence on the decoration of the interior.

What has been changed is the configuration of the original farmhouse to accommodate a more relaxed lifestyle. The proportions of the original dwelling have been altered dramatically with the conversion of several old outbuildings into guest cottages, and some rooms have been redesigned to make them fit for entirely new functions. For example, the original *cave*, or wine storage space, has been converted into an extra kitchen, the salon next door to it into a spacious kitchen and dining room, and a guest bedroom has taken over what was once the original kitchen. It is with this highly imaginative vision that the house has been allowed to expand and grow over time, restyled and modified according to different tastes and the individual and changing requirements that make for a comfortable lifestyle.

While despite, and indeed because of, various changes through the years the farmhouse has managed to retain its integrity as an original structure growing out of the surrounding landscape—fieldstone dressed with moss and lichen that is celebrated here has remained the most commonly used of all building materials throughout history—it nonetheless displays an imaginative, highly original view of country-house style.

The interior of the farmhouse boasts carefully thought-out details that bring the outside in, such as the simple fabrics in a palette of shades reflecting the countryside that have been used throughout for pillows, tablecloths, bed covers, and curtains, while the rich blue color of the wooden shutters—the wode that never fades which has for centuries been used across France as an effective insect repellent—pay tribute to the traditions born of the land. It is a home that has been lovingly created from the raw materials of the earth.

ABOVE LEFT The original *cave*, or wine store, has been turned into a second kitchen while still retaining ample storage for bottles of wine. The *cave* remains cool in the summer, making it ideal for food storage.

LEFT The walls around the side door are of rough stone, with courses of visible brick forming the door opening. Lemon trees grow in green-glazed terracotta pots.

OPPOSITE The house is ideally set up for outdoor living, with small seating areas strategically placed around the garden. The blue-painted shutters were originally painted with wode, which is a natural insect repellent. The 19th-century painted metal daybed is covered in cushions with fabrics designed by owner Kathryn Ireland. This region of France has inspired lines of her fabrics.

OPPOSITE The smooth walls of these village dwellings are made in the traditional way using a mixture of sand, small stones, and straw. They are painted off-white to reflect the relentless desert sun in the Berber hamlet of Timi Tagadert, which is 15 miles south of Marrakech, Morocco.

BELOW In this New Mexico adobe-style house, a covered courtyard veranda gives much-needed protection from the strong sunlight. The garden is a virtual zeriscape—all the plants chosen are natural to the environment.

earth

For thousands of years most regions have yielded an abundance of the soft, sedimentary rock known as clay. Country architecture historically looked for inspiration to the landscape—the materials to build with as well as the kind of agriculture practiced—and so cottages, farm-houses, lodges, and barns appear to spring from the land around them.

The soil has always provided a host of materials essential for building, including wood and stone, while the colors used to decorate both inside and out have traditionally reflected the life of the surrounding countryside: the cool shades of northern climates—the Netherlands, New England, and Scandinavia, for example—or the sizzling, vibrant hues that are typical of sunnier areas, ranging from New Mexico to Morocco and North Africa.

Among the materials that have been brought forth from the earth and which have continually taken pride of place for building is the humble brick. Used from antiquity, bricks are made by pressing brickearth—a form of clay—into a mold, which is then hardened by the processes of sun-drying or firing. Although the origins of brickmaking remain something of a mystery, sun-dried bricks have been discovered among the remains of neolithic structures at Jericho, and fired bricks are known to have been manufactured in the Indus Valley as far back as the third millennium B.C. Historically, brickmaking has tended to employ simple technology and minimize the need to transport materials by making use of the clay found in the soil at the

CLOCKWISE FROM TOP LEFT Near Santa Fe a door in a basalt dyke, built from lava covered with colored stucco, leads to a wild prairie. The ridge is a rock uplift that contains petroglyphs—early rock carvings—which are sacred to the Native Americans from this area.

In the same compound aspen trees provide extra shade. The house has a wraparound covered veranda that reveals a constant series of vistas, encouraging the owners to relax or eat outside sheltered from the sun.

At Domaine d'Heerstaayen in southern Holland, the native brick is covered with plaster.

This is one of the many buildings that make up the Tigmi Tagadert settlement, near Marrakech, Morocco. It is constructed in traditional fashion: the walls are made from sand, small stones, and straw and then painted, and the ceilings and balconies are made from wood taken from eucalyptus trees.

In Belgium the natural shape of massive tree trunks gives an unstructured look to the terrace.

In a riyad in the center of the medina in Marrakech, arches lead out to the traditional open-air central courtyard where an ornately tiled pool is surrounded by lemon trees.

site of construction. Bricks have always tended to be lightweight and fashioned in consistent shapes and sizes that are generally small enough to be picked up with one hand, thereby allowing a single workman to take charge of positioning and setting them in mortar. The texture, durability and color of the bricks depend upon the type of brickearth and additives used, alongside the firing temperatures and methods used for shaping.

Bricks have long been a reliable mainstay of country-house architecture. Well-worn kitchen floors, fireplace surrounds, and sun-baked terraces rendered in brick are equally at home in a humble country cottage nestled in the English Cotswolds or in a whitewashed Mediterranean villa on the southern coast of Spain. Durable as well as practical, surfaces created from brickwork lend a homespun rustic feel to the simple framework of a room, and marry comfortably with architectural features made from wood, such as ceiling beams, doors, or staircase banisters, as well as furnishing a lived-in backdrop for robust country-style tables, chairs, and bureaus.

Another dimension of earth-derived building materials and one that is closely related to the production of brick is terracotta—a decorative fabric produced by molding or modeling clay, which is then fired to create a hard and durable body that can be enhanced with colored paint or glazes and integrated into an architectural structure. The materials and techniques used to make terracotta resemble those employed in the production of brick, although terracotta clay generally tends to be more fine-grained and plastic than the raw material that makes up bricks, allowing for a depth of modeling

and delicately carved detail. Terracotta frequently boasts a hollow structure, whereas brick remains compact and solid. The surface of terracotta is often worked with tools to remove excess clay before firing, whereas bricks are generally molded and fired without additional polish, although they may occasionally be carved after firing. Terracotta that has been glazed is referred to as "faience," and from the middle of the 18th century until the 1850s, other forms of ceramic resembling terracotta, such as coade stone, were used to imitate stone surfaces. Terracotta and faience have always been valued for their resistance to the ravages of atmospheric pollution.

The wide-ranging history of terracotta includes the recorded use by the Babylonian culture from 1400 B.C., by the Asian subcontinent from the first millennium B.C. and by the Chinese, who produced decorated hollow stoneware blocks during the Han period (206 B.C. to A.D. 221). The ancient Greeks and Etruscans married painted terracotta ornament with constructions made from wood, and the Romans favored terracotta panels in low relief as decorative siding over brick. Although the practice of applying terracotta to buildings waned in Europe with the decline of the Roman Empire, it continued to flourish throughout Turkey, Persia, and Mogul India. The influence of Islamic techniques, and most significantly the addition of tin to glazes, resulted in the reintroduction of terracotta into Europe, where from the 14th century it was widely embraced once more, but this time for the creation of decorative ornament rather than as a construction material.

The rich, reddish-brown color of terracotta—it is the local clay of Tuscany and the name means "baked earth" in Italian—is especially well-

CLOCKWISE FROM TOP LEFT The essence of country can be achieved with less than perfect finishes. In this Belgian kitchen, a massive wooden table sits on terracotta tiles. The walls are roughly plastered and simple pickled wooden cupboards flank an ancient stone sink.
In Santa Fe the wall in the hallway has been painted a rough blue/green mix and then distressed. The owners like the dark feel as you enter, which leads the eye to windows beyond and breathtaking views of the mountains. The arched architecture of Morocco lends itself to small dark, intimate recesses where a guest can relax.

In hot climates, such as North Africa, the bedrooms are often kept light and cool. The ancient earth walls are tinted with natural pigment.
But in North Africa color is never far away. Stephen Skinner's Riyad Edward in Marrakech is close to the mosque of Side Bell Abbess in the northern Medina. The fireplace has a vivid blue base and a golden minaret top. The walls are easily formed into characteristic arches.
In the dining room of the adobe-style house near Santa Fe, the plaster walls have pigment injected into them and are then distressed using water. The floors are concrete tiles.

suited to country houses that have been built in warmer climates, such as those of the sunny Mediterranean—Provence, Andalusia, and Sicily. It is in the blazingly hot regions around the world—for example, the scorching southern coast of Spain which pays tribute to its North African heritage—where terracotta has featured as a key influence on country-house style, from the rich color of burnt sienna covering walls, floors paved with terracotta or quarry tiles, a host of terracotta pots lining a veranda, and the sun-baked red roof tiles that offer protection from the blistering rays of the sun.

And it is the age-old ceramic tile that rounds out the trio of building materials that have traditionally relied on the clay indigenous to the surrounding land. Unlike the bricks whose principal role is for construction, fired clay slabs, or tiles, have been used to weatherproof as well as decorate architecture since the third millennium B.C. Tiles are typically produced in molds to ensure uniformity of size and shape, then dried and fired in ceramic kilns. The majority of tiles are square in form, although roof tiles might also be circular or curvilinear, and decorative tiles originating in the Near East often adopted bold geometrical shapes—circles, four-cornered stars, diamonds, octagons, and triangles. The Moorish custom of using colorful tiles as a distinctive architectural feature eventually moved with the population shift to Spain and Portugal over the Straits of Gibraltar, where in country villas it was enthusiastically taken up to ornament floors, embellish walls, and to line kitchen and bedroom alcoves.

Most ceramic-producing cultures have traditionally made tiles. In addition to terracotta—the material generally favored for roof tiles and paving in ancient Rome as well as modern Italy and Spain—the blue-and-white tin-glazed Delftware of the 17th-century Netherlands, the sparkling lusterwares and brightly colored Isnik wares that have their origins in the Near East, and the luscious celadon, porcelain, and lead-glazed wares produced for centuries in East Asia—all have informed and inspired the

decoration of country houses spanning the globe, from a fire surround or backsplash above a kitchen sink in a humble Provençal cottage to the sun-drenched terrace, flamboyant arch, or a traditional Moorish-style bench that are typical of a sumptuous hacienda in the heart of Mexico.

Like any other clay form, tiles lend themselves to glazing and decoration that is usually confined to the exposed surface, which can be flat or deeply modeled by casting, molding, or carving. Country dwellings—from a stuccoed farmhouse surrounded by the sultry, hot climates of the southern Mediterranean to a large, luxurious sun-washed Spanish Colonial villa in Santa Fe—have traditionally been embellished with colorful tiles boasting eye-catching geometric decoration that pay tribute to the legacy of an exotic Arab heritage. Several ornamental techniques have been developed over the years that remain unique to tiles, such as *cuenca* —which look back to the 15th century and take their name from the Spanish word for "cell." This term refers to tiles that were impressed with raised edges forming a decorative pattern, and these channels were then filled with colored glazes, which became fluid when fired. The encaustic technique for tile decoration—revived on a large scale in the 19th century—describes a type of inlay that from the early 13th century was widely used throughout France and England, whereby a tile of red clay was stamped with a decorative design, then filled with white clay or slip and dipped in lead glaze before being fired. Tiles happily take to all kinds of glazes, although the more durable lead and ash glazes are favored for exposed surfaces. In general, wall tiles are usually glazed, while floor and roof tiles often remain unglazed. Other ornamental techniques for tiles include impressing and applied decoration.

Across the globe the spirit of the country home has traditionally embraced the earth and looked to the surrounding terrain for inspiration—often in conjunction with other natural materials, such as wood and stone. From the humble brick paving that borders the hearth of a cozy living room to a rooftop composed of plain, burnt sienna-colored terracotta tiles, and on to the brightly colored ceramic plaques painted with naïve designs that line a kitchen alcove—the earthen clay of the landscape has always provided not only a sense of warmth and comfort, but also what is both practical and functional about this rustic, homespun country style.

berber village

Known as the "Pearl of the South," the city of Marrakech in southwestern Morocco lies in the foothills of the imposing High Atlas Mountains. Moroccan architecture is inward looking—given to isolation and intimacy rather than ostentation. It offers enclosure and a place of contemplation and escape for its cloistered inhabitants.

ABOVE RIGHT Tigmi is in the hamlet of Tagadert south of Marrakech, Morocco. "Tigmi" means "my house" in Tashelhit; a Berber dialect used in the Haouz plain and the High Atlas Mountains. It is converted from a string of village dwellings.

BELOW While beautifully minimal, all areas at Tigmi are still steeped in the tradition of the area. At the same time the very simplicity gives the spaces a distinctly modern look.

Marrakech was founded around 1062 by Youssef bin Tachfine of the Almoravide dynasty, but it was his son Ali Ben Youssef who brought architects and craftsmen from Cordoba to build the mosques, palaces, and gardens to which the ancient city plays host. It also holds the largest Berber market—or souk—to be found in Morocco and the busiest square in all of Africa, called Djemaa el Fna. In 1126 the first circuit of walls were raised from *tabia*—the red mud of the plains. Like many other Middle Eastern cities, Marrakech has evolved over the centuries into two main divisions—the ancient medina and the modern city.

Perched on the brow of the Berber hamlet of Tagadert in the Haouz plain about 15 miles south of Marrakech and not far from the white-tipped peaks of the High Atlas Mountains, the greatest moutain range in North Africa, the tiny village of Tigmi boasts a population of little more than 200 inhabitants, most of whom are farmers. In the local Berber dialect of Tashelhit, the word Tigmi means dwelling or "my house." The central quarter of Tigmi was built in 1840 for Issa Abou Mehdi, the local judge.

It is into this picturesque setting that Max Lawrence arrived in 2001, purchasing a string of labyrinthine village houses with four courtyards. With the help of local artisan workers he set about lovingly renovating, restoring, and converting them into a single magnificent dwelling that he named Tigmi Tagadert. A welcome oasis of pale, cool colors situated against the backdrop of parched farmland, Tigmi Tagadert looks out over ancient mud walls to Oumnast—a colorful village dominated by a white kasbah—and to the High Atlas Mountains beyond.

Built in a style that is indigenous to this part of North Africa—the broad expanse of uneven walls punctuated with small doors and small window openings, and a roof comprised of split logs combined with branches—the house is organic and seems to grow naturally out of the countryside. The walls have been constructed according to traditional methods using recycled pisé—a type of reinforced mud that is a combination of sand, small stones, and straw—the floors are of limestone, while

OPPOSITE The massive organic shapes of the huge walls and staircases tower above an ancient doorframe and 19th-century doors. Reclaimed materials were sourced locally as locals preferred to replace old fixtures with new.

RIGHT Everywhere the relaxed nature of the building process is evident; the walls are gently curving, asymmetrical windows appear at random, and the stairs boast worn wooden treads. There is mystery in these halls and stairs—you never know quite where they might lead.

BELOW AND BELOW LEFT The ancient building techniques of North Africa can be adapted to suit modern demands. This shower room has walls covered in tadelakt—this was originally used to protect the surfaces of Moroccan *hammams* (the bath-houses) from moisture and keep them cool. This ancient technique where basic sand walls are "polished" with olive soap to a rich sheen can be reminiscent of marble or alabaster. The colors can be taken from the sand or introduced with pigments.

OPPOSITE In the main sitting area the huge ceiling, covered with eucalyptus, allows cooling breezes to fan the residents. These massive structural walls support the walkways and living rooms on the floors above.

the ceilings, balcony balustrades, and doors have been carved from logs taken from the fragrant native eucalyptus trees.

What is particularly striking is how the surrounding landscape plays such a pivotal role in the development and feel of the interior spaces. Corridors are open to the skies, and outdoor living is very much brought inside, with many sitting areas left open to the elements. The curved white walls proffer cool relief from the baking temperatures outside.

Country traditions also inform the decoration of the interior. All the building materials and textiles and pottery are made locally. Low wooden tables, iron and glass light fixtures, and colorful pottery are all locally made, and cushioned banquettes are covered with Berber textiles woven in Tigmi that are sprinkled with a vibrant palette of fuchsia, saffron, and orange. This connection with the Berber traditions transports the visitor into this country style that has changed little in centuries.

modern adobe

Not far from the state capital of New Mexico, the bustling city of Santa Fe—the name in Spanish means "Holy Faith"—lies the tiny village of Galisteo, where Ivy Ross and Brian Gill have created a light-filled, airy sanctuary that boasts a country simplicity that is at once both traditional and contemporary and clean lined.

Built with a flat roof in the historic Pueblo adobe style of architecture, the original house of the settlement forms the centerpiece of a one-story compound that comprises three buildings set around a gravel courtyard. The original house is in the middle of the compound, wrapping around a new-build guest house and a separate music and yoga retreat.

At an altitude of 6,500ft (2000m), the countryside surrounding Galisteo plays an important role in the way the house has evolved over time. Against a sapphire-blue sky spread endless vistas of the wide-open prairie lands that reach to the mountain ranges beyond—the Ortes, the San Juan, and the Sangre de Cristo ranges, which lie at the foothills of the Rockies. In front, the great expanses of the Galisteo basin are filled with low mesas with their scrubby forests of pinon, juniper, and sage brush. The play of sharp, strong rays of sunlight creates a pale palette of colors ranging from celery green and pink to gold, while the dramatic outlines of indigenous plants, including grasses, prickly cactus, and the stiff lance-like leaves of the yucca, punctuate the landscape. Brian has persuaded the local cattle ranchers to give him the yuccas and the stones covered with lichen which they need to clear from the land in order for their cattle to graze, to utilize for his compound.

It is against this distinctive background that this very contemporary-style adobe residence was built. At a cursory first glance everything looks totally traditional—the compound seems indistinguishable from its neighbors. But this is very much a modern architectural twist on the traditional sun-baked brick build. This passive solar construction is built from rastra—re-cycled polystyrene filled with concrete and rebar. In every instance the house has been constructed in an environmentally friendly manner—a 10,000 gallon (45,460kiloliter) cistern collects and recycles rain water, for example. The weather here

can change in an instant—a perfect blue sky can suddenly cloud over and torrential rain can deluge the property in minutes, and the cistern capitalizes on this natural phenomena. This area can even flood in the monsoon season.

To enter the main house from the dark entranceway to the slate terrace of the courtyard veranda—sheltered by a barraga, which gently diffuses the strong sunlight—one moves from the darkness into the light, with stunning views extending across the prairies to the mountains. Every room is bathed in the radiant glow that is typical of the southwest. In the main house the large living room boasts a white concrete floor and bare

ABOVE Lying low in the prairies in Galisteo, near Santa Fe in New Mexico, is the adobe-style home. There was an original structure that became the central element of a three-building compound.

OPPOSITE In the living area the walls are constructed of rastra, which is recycled styrofoam filled with concrete and rebar. It is passive solar. This is the 21st- century adobe! They are left undecorated—the windows provide an ever-changing tableau of the Galisteo basin to the Sandia and Rio Grande mountains beyond. The furniture is simple and geometric; the Springfield sofa, armchair, and tables are by Patricia Urquiola for Moroso.

LEFT The wraparound terrace allows vistas around the settlement. The monolithic nature of the construction, keeping to the local style of one-story building set into into the undulations of the land, fulfills the need to be part of the terrain, as well as a part of the tradition of native life.

ABOVE In the main living room of the main house the walls are plaster injected with pigment and then distressed with water to give a comfortable timeless feel. The painting here is entitled "Immeasurable Measure" and the table and chairs are by Brancusi.

OPPOSITE The distressed ocher of the walls and the simple concrete of the floor are bathed in light from the massive skylights above. They can be opened in summer for air, but here the weather can change very quickly. As you sit in the comfortable armchairs the brilliant blue sky can be peppered by small white clouds, which can quickly become "cloudbeings," as the Tewa call them, and then comes the wind from the north blowing the sage brush, and then torrential rain which can flood the property in the rainy season. Here there is an elemental reality to country living.

plaster walls in pale yellow that have been given a distressed look by injecting them with pigment and water, while skylights and four glass-paneled doors bring the outside inside and flood the space with shimmering golden sunlight. The importance of bringing light into the interior is also reflected in the choice of a clean-lined, ultra modern kitchen, with cabinets rendered primarily in aluminum—a splendid foil for the sunlight that pours through a generous expanse of window glass ranged across both the walls and the ceiling.

The native landscape is also mirrored in the furnishings of the main house, which are in simple, basic shapes and made of natural materials that echo the rich colors of the earth. Plain wooden tables, stools, and benches, native pottery, and the clean lines of framed prints ranged across the rustic mantelpiece afford the controlled but decorative embellishments. Throughout the house there are constant gentle reminders of the beauty and integrity of the countryside that lies beyond.

This theme of quiet simplicity is carried throughout the rest of the compound, with the plain, cube-shaped blocks of the interior spaces that define the concrete-walled guest house, which is given a decidedly modern twist in the choice of beds, sofas, and chairs in a rainbow of bright lollipop colors.

belgian brick

The country lifestyle is celebrated close to the Belgian border where south of Breda in Holland lies the farm and vineyard known as Domaine d'Heerstaayen, owned by the enterprising Peter and Marijke de Wit. They have reclaimed the farmhouse from the cows that were living in it to create a beautiful home surrounded by a wonderful garden.

ABOVE To many people the country idyll consists of owning an old brick house covered in climbing roses or vines, with acres of neatly tended gardens and perhaps your own vineyard. Well, in Breda in South Holland, Peter and Marijke de Wit have acheived just that. But this country idyll has taken 25 years of hard work; creating a vineyard in Holland was no easy task.

RIGHT The mellowed old brick walls of the farm, built in 1915, create the perfect outside dining room with a covered canopy. This house is very much about being outside and enjoying the views of the garden and the neat and prolific rows of vines.

LEFT A blissful old brick walkway with box hedge "rooms" filled with vegetables, herbs, and flowers is surrounded again with old brick walls. Country is also about smells: the lavender, mint, and rosemary, the box plants themselves, the grapes when they are harvested.

ABOVE In a small arbor sturdy wooden chairs allow a moment's respite from toiling in the gardens.

RIGHT The old farm and stable had stood empty for many years and required complete renovation; old doors were utilized where possible, and new windows in harmonious style were painted in a gray blue paint. The outside is wrapped in greenery, and the vines are ever present. Peter grows varieties such as Pinot Noir, Pinot Gris, Chardonnay, Riesling, and late-ripening vines such as Cabernet and Merlot.

The farmhouse lifestyle enjoyed by Peter and Marijke de Wit has roots in Peter's interest in the production of wine, which dates to the late 1960s, when he first traveled to France to work at several chateaux in the Bordeaux region. By 1979, he had realized his dream to create and manage a vineyard when he planted in Dutch soil his first Pinot Noir vines that he had brought from Gevrey-Chambertin. This initial endeavor met with great success and was soon followed by the addition of six varieties of grapes including Pinot Gris, Chardonnay, Riesling, and even late-ripening vines such as Cabernet and Merlot, which continue to be produced at the vineyard today.

In 1998 Peter and Marijke purchased an old run-down farm not far from their neighboring vineyard, and with characteristic vision, energy, and enthusiasm they set about renovating it. Built in 1915, the farm had not kept up with the times and was discovered by the de Wits to be in a hopelessly neglected and ramshackle state. There remained in the house, for example, the stable where the cows had at one time lived and a bathroom, kitchen, and central heating were conspicuous by their absence. Faced with the daunting task of making this forsaken house habitable once more, Peter and Marijke devoted the next five years to lovingly bringing it back to life.

Everything about this charming farmhouse pays tribute to the surrounding landscape. With the addition of a fireplace, the de Wits converted the stable that once was home to the cows into a spacious and hospitable living room—with heating furnished by pipes for running hot water being placed inside the original clay and straw walls—as well as opening up two small rooms to create an expansive area for dining. Throughout the house the atmosphere is warm and welcoming, with planked walls painted in cool creamy neutral colors to bring in the light, exposed ceiling beams, and floors constructed with

RIGHT On a wonderfully patterned old herringbone brick floor, two old pine racks on castors provide perfect storage; whether it is for shoes or freshly baked bread.

BELOW In the kitchen, the black range takes central stage. Most people who have owned a stove like this insist it is the essential ingredient of a country kitchen.

OPPOSITE The old farm and stable needed sensitive restoration to make a comfortable country home. The floors have herringbone brickwork and tiles. The tongue-and-groove walls were painted a warm yellow, and the house filled with country furniture. The large painted glazed cupboard adds a touch of the classic to this high-ceilinged room.

flagstones or faced with herringbone-patterned brick left bare. Furniture is simple, practical, and spare in natural materials reflecting the time-honored country-house tradition. The room kitchen with an Aga range reflects the country-style aesthetic, but interprets it in a thoroughly modern way.

The outside of Domaine d'Heerstaayen is as pleasing and comforting as the interior of the house. Just as they had done with the barn that is used for the production of the wine, Peter and Marijke created the Orangerie, for wine tastings as well as dining, from an old barn originally intended for keeping pigs—with brick walls, wooden plank doors and shutters the color of the bright blue sky, and a glass conservatory roof that bathes the plants inside with light. The lavish garden is a wholly original conception that has been created from the surrounding meadows and paved with local cobbled stone and boasting a sumptuous carpet of flora consisting of trees, pots of herbs, and a luscious array of flowers, plants, and vines punctuated with a number of shaded sanctuaries for reading, visiting, enjoying the vista or sampling a glass of the local wine.

In this remote area of the Netherlands, Peter and Marijke de Wit have managed to build a splendid country sanctuary that is the essence of simplicity, while in every way honoring the materials and colors found in the surrounding landscape.

a sense of place

france

In concert with country dwellings across the globe, rural houses in France have for centuries forged a close bond with their surroundings, incorporating local materials in their construction and reflecting the colors of the landscape in their decoration. And it is the region of Provence in the southeastern corner of the country that best sums up the French interpretation of country style.

It is color that most clearly defines the spirit of the French taste for country living. Beneath a brilliant sun in a pale sapphire sky lies the exuberant palette found in the trees, plants, and flowers of the Provençal valley landscape—which is nestled between the River Rhone and the Mediterranean Sea. Generous fields of lemon-yellow sunflowers, bright cherry-red poppies, and golden wheat form a vivid contrast to towering cypress, olive, or chestnut trees, lush vineyards, and meadows filled with the heady fragrance of pale purple lavender. The beguiling palette of intense and sumptuous earth colors that seduced the painter Vincent van Gogh in the late 19th century—russet, ocher, and pale apricot, butter yellow, blues ranging from faded sky to turquoise, and the silvery shades of emerald and moss green—continue to touch the imagination even today.

Provençal country style owes much to the traditional farmhouse—essentially a weathered warm stone or clay-built *mas* designed to resist the unrelenting sun and the harsh winds of the mistral—that boasts a flat roof built of red clay tiles along with window shutters and well-sized doors brightly painted with a rainbow of vibrant colors inspired by the surrounding countryside—sunshine yellow, burnt orange, and grass green. The outside is brought indoors as well, with the characteristic lofty ceilings and thick walls either whitewashed or plastered and colorwashed in tones that reflect the natural shades of the landscape—from the soft buff of the local stone and clay to the sharp mustard and mellow rust of the fields beyond.

The bold colors and bright patterns found in the rich, fertile landscape also shape the informal atmosphere of the Provençal farmhouse interior—a medley of shiny tiles in vivid shades of green, yellow, and crimson that line a fireplace surround, a kitchen floor laid in a checkerboard of vibrant red

and green, a wooden door washed in a brilliant cobalt blue, or a corner cupboard painted daffodil yellow. Having their distant origins in the Indian cottons that passed through the busy port of Marseilles with the East India Company in the 17th century, the locally produced characteristic fabrics, printed with geometric, fruit, and flower patterns against brightly colored backgrounds of beige, scarlet, and citrus yellow, remain synonymous with the countryside of southern France today

Coupled with the countryside, the Mediterranean and its ports have played a pivotal role in the evolution of Provençal style. From the 18th century the sea attracted a legion of artists and craftsmen who took inspiration not only from the colors of the landscape, but also from the exchange of ideas brought from beyond its shores. As a result, this rural pocket in southern France has long played host to a company of highly skilled and

ABOVE Jean-Louis Raymond and Kenyon Kramer have converted a sleepy farmhouse into a charming cottage. The color of the stone, painted shutters, and exterior stone slabs are the essence of Provence.

OPPOSITE AND BELOW This stone farmhouse was built in the 1820s in farmland near St. Rémy in the South of France. The garden is as important as the interior, with its old trees, topiary, and a broad terrace with bay trees, a canopy of vines, and a table set for lunch in the dappled sunlight.

LEFT In Kenyon Kramer's kitchen in his pavillion in the South of France, a large wooden hutch covered with distressed paint houses the dishes and glassware.

OPPOSITE This is a typical Provençal kitchen, with an 18th-century stone fireplace and a Belgian slate floor. The archetypal French Lacanche stove is surrounded by an array of copper pans. This kitchen/eating area is the heart of any French home, from Normandy to Alsace, from Lorraine to the Midi-Pyrénées.

BELOW In France, the muted earth colors of the north contrast with the brighter palette of Provence.

talented artisans who left their creative mark on decorative furnishings, in particular furniture and textiles. Today, country style looks to these past customs for inspiration—furniture that for wealthier households usually consisted of oak, pine, or beechwood cupboards, chairs, sideboards, and the general-purpose armoires made of local walnut that were frequently carved with patterns of fruit and foliage—or more cheaply painted with ribbons of fruits and flowers—and complemented with modest furniture such as plain kitchen tables, box-framed beds, rush-seated chairs, and simple benches.

But alongside 21st-century interpretations of the age-old farmhouse style of Provence—be it a newly built cottage or a sleek modern apartment—that embrace the tradition of sturdy, hard-wearing furniture punctuated with sizzling colors and richly patterned textiles can be found imaginative versions that boast a highly original modern twist. The cozy and warm ambience of the refuge-providing country-house interior also rejoices in the inspired and sophisticated combinations of

modern colors, materials, and textures with more traditional ones—concrete walls that share space with timeworn wooden beams, for example; reclaimed doors and tables that have been married with seagrass carpets; suede, linen, and cashmere upholstery and window curtains in soft color schemes—taupe, gray, buff—and decorative details, including tiles in pale muted shades and hard-edged renderings of vernacular furniture—commodes, chairs, and armoires—in modern materials such as cast-aluminum, fiberglass, plastic, and Lucite.

At the heart of French country style lies the practical, purposeful farmhouse kitchen, which owes much of its charm to a range of simple furnishings designed for the storage and preservation of food and to the custom of having the equipage on display—dishes, carving knives, and copper pans. These happily mingle with a variety of materials—the rough-hewn stone of a generously proportioned fireplace, the patina of well-worn wooden tables and chairs, glossy china in bright shades of sunshine yellow and emerald green, and vividly patterned cotton

tablecloths, seat covers, and curtains—to create a warm and comfortable retreat. Of course, the cozy ambience of the country-house interior need not necessarily rely solely upon such time-honored traditions. Gleaming pots and pans made from stainless steel, sleek refrigerators, and sophisticated clean-lined stoves give a nod to the country lifestyle while acknowledging the modern need to be efficient and practical.

Dining out-of-doors is an essential part of life in the South of France, and ways of reclaiming in the modern world the informality and warm comfort of country life that is a hallmark of the Provençal farmhouse tradition include the creation of a shaded, brick-paved terrace that is lined with orange trees, box topiary, and terracotta pots planted with a rich patchwork of herbs such as thyme and rosemary—all of which can be equally at home in the sweeping expanse of a lush garden in France or bordering the cast-iron railings of a tiny balcony perched high above the busy urban streets of Manhattan.

The charm of the Provençal way of life continues to resonate today, with a decorative style that looks to the country for inspiration but remains one that refuses to be locked into the idea of faithfully mirroring every last detail from the past. Whether alive with the traditional bright colors and spirited patterns that pay homage to the surrounding landscape, or softened by the warm and weathered shades found in the bleached clay and stones of the countryside—the modern interior that seeks to provide warmth and comfort and a refuge from the stresses of modern life need look no farther than a farmhouse nestled in the hillsides of southern France.

RIGHT In an 18th-century *manoir* (manor house) in the Dordogne, a guest bedroom has wide chestnut floorboards, original to the house, a distressed paint finish on the walls, and a four-poster bed painted in traditional style by local paint artist Liz Sangster. The small bed stool is carved from 19th-century French fruitwood. In the past it was quite common to have stools set next to four-poster beds, which were normally high off the ground to protect the sleeper from drafts, vermin, and "night vapors."

OPPOSITE In a Normandy *relais de poste* (coaching inn) built circa 1830, the massive A-frame roof truss is exposed in the guest bedroom. The brick floor is also original to the building. The distressed white walls and muted colors draw the eye to the grand 19th-century oil painting over the bed.

RIGHT In both of these cottages in Provence, *toile de Jouy* fabric is used to create a classic French look. *Toile de Jouy* fabrics originated in a factory established in 1770 in the French village of Jouy-en-Josas by the German Oberkampf brothers. They had discovered advances made in England in copperplate printing techniques. This allowed them to produce these pictorial fabrics in much larger quantities, mainly printed in single colors. Madder (red) was one of the first to be produced and is still popular today. Many companies produce documentary fabrics from these original designs.

italy

There is nothing that conjures up the warmth, comfort, generosity, and relaxation that lies at the heart of a truly satisfying country aesthetic better than the productive hills of Italy's Tuscan and Umbrian provinces, with their terraced vineyards, tall cypress trees, and expansive olive groves.

ABOVE The russet-colored farmhouse of Macennere Alto, in Tuscany, is surrounded by espaliered lemon trees, and terraced olive groves. From the house, the tented pool house—a series of columns hung with white linen curtains—looks like a Greek temple.

These vine-clad hills with small hill towns perched precariously on top capture the essence of country escape: the simplicity, security, romance, and refuge. The universal appeal of Italian country can be traced to its essential simplicity. Low-built from local stone and clad in sun-bleached pink or golden ocher stucco, Tuscan houses have traditionally been built to be both comfortable and cool, boasting generous proportions, thick rough-plastered walls, well-trodden floors paved with brick or tile, high-beamed ceilings, and slatted shutters to gently bring the rays of the sun inside. The roof is often covered with rows of terracotta tiles, a design left over from the architects of ancient Rome. In fact, this is one of the great strengths of Italian country style—the fact that it appears to be seamlessly tied to the past. These ancient houses have seen the passing of centuries as they sit under the Tuscan sun. There is no recognition of or allowance

RIGHT In the dining area, an antique distressed-wood cabinet is juxtaposed with new chairs painted in black, white, and gray.

BELOW A pair of black lamps frame a painting on this chest of drawers in one of the bedrooms. By night, these lamps illuminate the room's pale washed walls to provide an intimate ambience.

Rich expanses of color that take inspiration from the warm glow and sumptuous hues of surrounding landscape—weather-beaten terracottas, yellow ochers, and the burnt sienna that takes its name from the red clay hills surrounding the hilltop town of Sienna—are lavishly applied to cover walls and ceilings. Not for these walls the dictates of flat color. The local pigments soak into the wet plaster just as they did with the great fresco painters. The resultant finish is warm and comfortable and relaxing to the eye. During the daytime the warmth of these dry earthy colors absorbs the heat, and then return it to the rooms after sunset. Rooms for the afternoon siesta are painted in cool fresh shades taken from the herbs that can be found across the Tuscan countryside—the green of thyme, the faded gray-blue of lavender. Today the color palette borrowed from the tonal landscape of Tuscany and Umbria brings into a modern interior the same satisfying atmosphere of comfort and relaxation, as it mirrors at once its character of affable warmth as well as a sense of serenity and wellbeing. Here, long sun-drenched days are to be enjoyed rather than hidden from. Shutters keep rooms cool, but the sun is allowed in to cast long shadows and add warmth to the delicious Tuscan and Umbrian colors.

Although traditionally built on a generous scale, the Tuscan country house remains generally uncluttered and sparely furnished, with chairs, tables, and cupboards typically arranged around the walls of the rooms—a feature that is largely due to its architectural structure, which sweeps from room to room, through broad doorways and spacious arches, moving from the inside to the outside. The result is an ambience that is more formal than that found in the country dwellings of England ar

ABOVE An antique sleigh bed bought in England and enlarged by Matthew Collins adorns one of several bedrooms in this rustic farmhouse.

RIGHT This small bathroom has been enlivened with Ultramarine Violet pigment from Nutshell.

for our modern world of stress and chaos. This style has outlived the vagaries of Baroque and the Rococo of rich men's foibles—Italian country style is timeless and unconcerned with the constantly changing goal-posts of modern design. This is not to say that the modern world has to be totally excluded—these homes can easily adapt to modern furnishings, because this is a forgiving and all-encompassing style.

The outdoors also plays an important role in the life of an Italian country house. Red-brown terracotta—the local clay of Tuscany—flags an expansive sun-baked terrace lined with flower-filled terracotta urns and lemon trees where dining in the open air is a fundamental part of the rural lifestyle of Italy. The smells, too, are redolent of warm summer carefree days—the herbs, the lavender, the freshly brewed coffee, the freshly baked bread, the deep aroma of olive oil, and the hint of garlic in the air. And the sounds: the tractor in the fields, the buzz of the honey bees, the call of the cicadas, the gentle trickle of water from the village fountain, the pop of a cork—all add to the hypnotic effect that is Italian country style.

France, where furniture is usually scattered around the center of the room. This kind of formality suits not only a Tuscan farmhouse, but it is equally at home in a modern interpretation of Italian country style, such as a high-rise apartment with small-sized rooms that requires a minimum of furniture.

Typically, the furniture found in an Italian country house is of simple construction, and usually rendered in local ... Rustic wooden chests, cupboards, and hutches made by craftsmen tend to be left in the honeyed tones of the wood or occasionally given a coat of paint, although timber is frequently camouflaged by an age-old known as *arte povera*—where flowers and landscapes are imitation of the elaborate inlaid work of more furniture. Among other decorative features that bring rm to Tuscan country living include the use of on, which is formed into elaborately curled bed nd ornate window grilles. Built-in furniture is relatively mon, with the exception of shelves or small cupboards. rative furnishings also tend to be quite plain. Unglazed

terracotta pots and urns are filled with colorful flowers or dried herbs. Fabrics tend to eschew floral patterns in favor of checks and stripes in bold combinations of yellow with blue or red and green. Beds boast loose woven covers in pale creamy tones, along with filmy, diaphanous gauze fabrics to hang around them, and windows are almost never curtained, which brings the golden light and lush rolling hills of the Tuscan countryside in. The warm, weathered shades of the walls are picked up in faded woven tapestries, colorful embroidered cushions and pillows, and handcrafted kelims.

The warm mellow mood of the Italian style of the country easily adapts to the 21st-century desire for a relaxing and comfortable refuge from the pace of modern life. Tuscan country style is equally at home in a fashionable contemporary apartment in Paris, a Georgian townhouse in the heart of London, or in a sunwashed villa nestled in the Arizona desert, sharing and celebrating the sunshine-filled pleasures of rural Italy with rough-walled, sparsely furnished rooms bathed in the warm terracotta and ocher hues that define Italian country style.

ABOVE Country palettes have traditionally depended on the pigments from the surrounding earth. Italy has always been associated with the rich colors of the fresco painters: terracotta, ochers, and a myriad of blue tones.

ABOVE LEFT The rustic nature of this Tuscan farmhouse is echoed in the wooden rafters and simple entrance hall, which is painted bright, welcoming yellow.

scandinavia

In the isolated communities of Sweden's scattered provinces, it is the farmhouse that defines Scandinavian country style, along with interior decoration that pays tribute to the abundant forests and reflects the cool clear palette of colors that can be found in the surrounding countryside.

ABOVE In this mountainous area of Norway, the wooden cabins hug the land. They are built low in the terrain to protect the structure from the severe winters. The roof covered in grasses further blends the building into the landscape and provides a form of natural central heating.

RIGHT In Sweden white-painted contemporary Gustavian-style chairs are based on country examples of these iconic late 18th-century chairs. The off-white tied covers are an attractive and practical modern twist. A quilt covers the table. The brick floor is original to the building.

LEFT These massive neoclassical columnar stoves were popular all over Scandinavia; they were typically decorated with tin-glazed earthenware floral tiles to complement the Gustavian palette.

RIGHT Old wooden containers (treen) are common to all the Scandinavian countries. This is filled with clovers and other wildflowers from the Hardangervidda, the highest mountain plain in northern Europe.

BELOW The Scandinavian palette typically includes pale blues, grays, off-whites, and pinks. This Gustavian chair, decorated with carved floral decoration, is a direct copy of a French 18th-century example. Sweden was not as wealthy as France, and hence it is painted rather than gilded, which is one of the reasons why it is more in demand for today's country interiors.

For centuries, the rural landscape—dotted with lakes and surrounded by mountains and forests—coupled with a climate of long harsh winters has largely shaped the style of the typical Scandinavian country dwelling. The plentiful supply of lumber has ensured that wood for building has held sway both inside and out, with large-scale farmhouses commonly boasting thick, heavy log walls, open fireplaces, massive doors, and paneling. Rustic country furniture made from pine was traditionally painted or carved and fretted with folk motifs.

The thread of Scandinavian style known as Gustavian is especially appealing for the 21st-century country interior—whether an apartment in the heart of Stockholm or a farmhouse in rural New England. This style, which combines simplicity with a love for decoration—borne from a long love affair with French taste and fashion that had begun in the 17th century and was enthusiastically promoted in the late 18th century by the culturally aware monarch Gustav III—eventually found its way from the grand houses of the aristocracy into the more modest dwellings of rural farmers. The rustic strand of the Swedish country style adapted to the new fashion by bringing into the interior provincial adaptations of more stylish French furniture.

Swedish country style is all about comfort, calm, and relaxation. There is a sense of lightness, an airy feel and purity about the Gustavian interior, which adopts a simpler, more pastoral flavor than does its flamboyant French cousin. Rooms typically are ample and well-proportioned but sparsely furnished; they often feature a tiled stove, with the abundant woods of Scandinavia used to create an uncomplicated, ordered, and quietly elegant atmosphere. Although the furnishings of a Gustavian interior were heavily influenced by the neoclassical style of France during the reign of Louis XVI, they tend even today to boast a modesty and restraint that is typical of their

ABOVE The logs are painted a soft green taken from the colors outside this Norwegian cabin. The flowers grow on mountain marshes. They are called *engsmelle,* or maidens' tears.

OPPOSITE This planked kitchen/dining area was built onto a small log cabin in the Oslo fjord. Everything is kept neutral and light. The 19th-century table and old-style painted chairs are softened by the use of fabrics, which pick up the tones from the plates with Finnish scenes in the rack above.

BELOW When the exteriors of homes are dark wood and the winter days are short, it is common in Scandinavia to find either interiors painted with colors taken from the surroundings or, as here, with tones of white.

northern heritage. For example, gilding is eschewed in favor of plain white, pale yellow, or gray paint—and while the clean-lined shapes and classical decorative ornament of chairs and sofas reflect French influence, the Swedish interpretation tends to be simpler and more pared down. Rustic furnishings that were designed with an eye to saving space—beds and cupboards built into walls, chests and stoves tucked into corners—still resonate for the modern space-starved interior today. Fabrics are made of hearty woven linens in check and stripe patterns rather than of the delicate silk preferred by the French.

The frosty Scandinavian palette found in the surrounding landscape dictates the hues that have been chosen to decorate the rooms of a country-inspired dwelling. The Gustavian style of Sweden traditionally favors a host of various shades of cream, white, and off white along with pearl gray that happily mix with the soft colors of local flora such as yellow and green grasses and the pale pink or pale blue of roses and harebells. In

an effort to maximize the available light during the long dark winter months, rooms feature tall windows that have been hung with fine cotton curtains in white or pale colors. Woodwork is often painted off-white with bare wide floorboards of scrubbed pine left uncovered, stripped to reveal the muted natural tones of the wood or occasionally featuring decorative inlaid patterns.

The muted color palette of the Swedish countryside is also taken up in the fabrics and wall treatments of the interior. Walls and wall paneling are typically painted white and sometimes outlined in blue or pink following Gustavian tradition, covered with printed wallpapers, or stripped to the natural color of the wood. Canvas wall hangings painted with garlands of fruits and flowers are another traditional feature that is popular today.

The Scandinavian sensibility shares with the American in particular a preference for marrying the old with the new to create a distinctive and appealing home. Rejecting the familiar image of the cluttered country cottage, this ideal of the country style frequently finds an older, even rustic dwelling that has been brought to life with a thoroughly modern interior. While a solidly built farmhouse or cottage that boasts a rich history might be attractive and full of charm, for many the idea of escaping to a cozy refuge does not necessarily include surrounding oneself with a hodge-podge of decorative antique bibelots, a jumble of kitchenware and cooking pots, piles of pillows and blankets, collections of old china and glass, shelves of books, and a random scattering of plants.

Rather, a more modern take on the meaning of escape often takes hold, one that finds solace and comfort in freedom from needless encumbrances. With imagination and sensitivity, the rooms of a relatively old house might be simply and sparsely furnished and decorated in a thoroughly contemporary style—post-war linear designs made of modern materials such as rubber, aluminum, and plywood, glass-topped pedestal tables, leather-covered lounge chairs and sofas, curtain-free windows, perhaps a scatter rug or two, and a single painting or photograph to bring a splash of color to a room that has been painted in pale cool shades. This is the Scandinavian country

OPPOSITE In the original part of this cabin built in 1925 in northwestern Norway, the various blue and white fabrics on the corner daybed relieve the dark walls. As the cabin is now surrounded by the waters of the Oslo fjord the fabrics mirror the views from the windows.

RIGHT The traditional bed for a Scandinavian log cabin is a *himmelseng*, or heaven bed. It completely encases you and can take up most of the space in the bedroom, which for warmth tended to be quite small. This bed in a wooden lodge near Lillehammer is based on the original, but is more delicate, lighter and more spacious than the original.

BELOW The style of this small concrete and tile fireplace in the corner of a small sitting room in Norway is traditional.

BELOW RIGHT The northern palette owes much to the Gustavian period in late 18th-century Swedish history, with its cold off-whites, grays, and pale blues. These were warmed by tones of pink and rose. In rural areas stone and green tones were also used.

ideal brought into the 21st century, one that offers comfort and relaxation from an ever more complicated world. It is a style that has enormous and enduring appeal and unlimited potential. The extensive use of white and muted pale colors or faded natural woods, the cool, clear approach to space with an uncluttered scattering of furnishings boasting simple clean lines invite the feeling of calm and a sense of comfort and relaxation that are fundamental both to the country aesthetic and a modern approach to decorating. Whether it is a log cabin on a Colorado mountain, a cottage nestled on the Irish coast, or a sleek minimalist apartment in an Italian palazzo, the Scandinavian tradition offers a fitting backdrop for accommodating the taste for the rustic spirit of the countryside as well as a more modern interpretation of the ageless Gustavian aesthetic.

united kingdom

For many, it is the English countryside and the small cluttered thatch-roofed cottage constructed from stone and surrounded by roses and hollyhocks that embodies the romantic ideal of the rural past and sets the standard for the country house style. This traditional low-ceilinged abode, with its reassuringly solid walls, was the customary home of rural inhabitants for centuries.

ABOVE Quintessentially English, an 18th-century Cotswold stone house nestles around its country garden.

BELOW Specially chosen artifacts can create the perfect cameo for a country room. This workbench, used by an itinerant cobbler in Wales at the end of the 18th century, holds a French shore-bird decoy, a butter pail, butter stamps, French leather shoes circa1860, and 19th-century clogs.

OPPOSITE All the elements in this 18th-century village house kitchen add up to the feeling of English country; the terracotta tiles on the floor, the butcher's block on wheels, the wrought-iron hanging unit and, of course, the white Aga range.

In the mind's eye the simplicity and comfort that lies at the heart of the English rural idyll proffers the consummate solution for escape from the hectic pace of the 21st-century lifestyle, and it is the cramped cottage that conjures up the image of a perfect hideaway. The surrounding landscape—with its verdant rolling hills, forests, hedgerows, fields, and meadows—along with the whimsical climate has shaped and colored the character of English architecture, which tends to wear a timeworn weathered patina on roofs, weathered doors, and window shutters. Relaxed and informal, the cottage interior typically is a higgledy-piggledy arrangement of small rooms where every possible inch of space has been used to advantage, a style of agreeable confinement where books and pottery, tables, beds and chairs, toys, and copper pots and pans cheerfully jumble together.

The decoration of a country cottage is practical as well as comfortable, and the somewhat simple handling of the walls,

ceilings, and floors is key to the intrinsic appeal of the country style. To bring light into utilitarian rooms such as the kitchen, the rough plasterwork walls might be painted with a palette of pale colors—faded ocher, rich cream, buttermilk, and egg-yolk yellow—and occasionally embellished with stenciled patterns. In other rooms wall paneling might be shaded in the dull faded greens, cloudy blues, and grays or in the deep muddy-brown and brick earth tones that bring the outside in by reflecting the palette of the surrounding landscape, while walls constructed of brick or stone tend to be limewashed in the soft whispering hues of peach, golden yellow, or pink. Floors that are made of wooden planks, brick, quarry tiles, or flagstones are usually left bare, covered with simple rush matting or with a random sprinkling of colorful painted floorcloths and hooked rugs. The woodwork of a country cottage—plank doors, window frames, and ceiling beams—might boast the rich, timeworn patina of the natural wood, left in a distressed state to show the passage of time or painted with natural earth tints, including traditional seaweed green or duck's-egg blue.

The outdoors also plays a key role in the cottage interior for the decorative wallpapers and textile furnishings that take inspiration from the archetypal English cottage garden. A romantic as well as a vibrant hodge-podge of old-fashioned flowers—climbing roses, foxgloves, pansies, marigolds, lupines and sweet peas among them—turn up on block-printed cotton curtains, quilted coverlets, and crewelwork pillows.

The practical nature of an English cottage can be observed with a look at its furniture, for nothing is superfluous and unnecessary. Traditionally made by local craftsmen from indigenous wood—elm, oak, pine, ash, and sycamore—to designs that over the centuries have remained relatively static, country-style furniture tends to be sturdy and relatively plain

appealing today. By its very nature it offers the ideal sanctuary from the anxiety and burdens that form a fundamental part of life in the 21st century because nothing about it tries too hard or looks for perfection. This is a taste that sits comfortably with a contemporary interpretation—whether for a modern city apartment, a Victorian townhouse, or a small farmhouse nestled in the countryside. The success of the English country idiom lies with what is essentially its magpie character, an eclectic mixture of different styles from different periods, well-loved and timeworn furniture, robust textiles and decorative objects, and the confident use of color to create a harmonious whole.

The tradition of the English country lifestyle does not, however, remain stubbornly fixed in the past. Although there remains tremendous respect and reverence for what has gone before, many of those who embrace the country aesthetic and celebrate the idea of a comfortable refuge from the stresses of modern life do not by choice rely for solace upon vibrantly colored chintz upholstery, a mishmash of ornamental decorative objects, or old furniture that bears the marks and scars of repeated use over many years. The search for the nurturing comfort that in hearts and minds is synonymous with old English country resonates in the 21st century in spare, clean-lined dwellings that look both back for inspiration to the past—

ABOVE These Gothic-style windows are typical of many buildings in Britain in the late 18th to early 19th century. Country style can also cross national boundaries—although quintessentially Cotswold style, the shutters are French, as is the fabric on the very English armchair.

RIGHT Country furniture was not always rustic in appearance. This English painted hutch from circa 1770 has fine architectural pilasters, showing a high quality design. It is hard to find furniture with good original paintwork like this—the Prussian-blue pigment was mixed with casein (a milk-based medium). This again is a sign of quality; Prussian blue was an expensive pigment in the 18th century.

but above all useful. Purpose-built cupboards, beds, and chests, armoires, sideboards and Welsh hutches, tables, and ladderback, slatback or English Windsor chairs, spice cabinets, built-in closets and stoves for cooking—all have a function and a place.

For the country cottage, furniture tended to be produced in provincial adaptations of more fashionable versions that were typically rendered in mahogany or walnut. Many pieces were painted to add light and color to the interior as well as to disguise any flaws in the wood. As with woodwork, with the passage of time, furniture that has been painted takes on a weathered patina that is very much at home in a country-style interior. Baskets suspended from the ceiling for holding herbs, colorful crockery for eating, lamps for lighting, quilts and coverlets for keeping warm, walls lined with shiny copper pots for cooking, milk pitchers for displaying a bunch of wildflowers, and hooks for hanging everything from coats to teacups are at once decorative as well as practical. No space is wasted, and it is this pragmatic spirit that highlights the charm of country style.

There is a lived in, comfortable, and seemingly random eccentricity about the English country cottage that is enormously

BELOW English country can transcend the cluttered cottage look. Today you are more likely to find a cool minimal approach to the design—with whites, off-whites, grays, and mushroom on the walls and sea grass on the floors. The color is brought to the room by the French ticking on the comfortable armchairs.

from the sparsely furnished medieval interior to the unfussy lines and distinctive lack of ornamental artefacts favored by the Arts and Crafts practitioners in the late 19th century—as well as ahead to a future that was initially shaped by the Modernists.

For many people across the centuries, relaxation and escape lie in what is minimal and uncomplicated, and yet what gives the English its unique country character is the ability to combine the old and the new, to celebrate the richness and the warmth of the Tudors along with the angular, sharp shapes and novel materials found in the spare modern style championed by pioneers such as Frank Lloyd Wright, Charles and Ray Eames, Marcel Breuer or Mies van der Rohe in the U.S., Le Corbusier at the Bauhaus, or the visionary Finn Alvar Aalto.

LEFT The palette of England is the palette of the landscape—the green of the hills and the earth colors of the fields. This light palette consists of ivories, creams, and faded greens, with a splash of warm rose.

north america

Developed from a rich and evocative amalgam of the old and the new, the heritage of the native tribes mingled with the skills and traditions brought from all over Europe by the first settlers, who readily utilized the wealth of indigenous materials available to them, American country style today continues to celebrate the independent and creative spirit of those early pioneers.

ABOVE This classic 1765 saltbox house in Litchfield County, Connecticut, is painted in shades of taupe. In the 1840s Andrew Jackson Downing wrote that houses should be painted "in shades of gray . . . and drab or fawn color, which will be found pleasing and harmonious in any section of the country."

The distinctive nature of American country interiors owes much to the astonishing variety of regional styles that grew up in the isolated rural communities that were established from the 17th century on by the very first pioneers. From the houses built by the Amish, the Shakers, the Pennsylvania Dutch, and the New Englanders, among others, evolved a melting-pot style that came to be seen as uniquely American in character.

As with most of the interpretations of country style that span the globe, it is the colors and materials found in the local landscape that initially provide inspiration. From its beginnings the primary source for building materials across the new continent—ranging from the rolling hills of the Midwest to the fertile lands of the deep South—were the abundant timber-rich forests that yielded an impressive assortment of lustrous indigenous woods. Cherry, elm, pine, ash, birch, poplar, hickory, and maple vied with cypress in the southern regions and the

white cedar found on the Atlantic coast for the construction of houses—roofs, sidings, and shingles, doors, and shutters—as well as for structure of the interior—wall paneling, floorboards, a staircase, and ceiling beams. Today the taste for the country continues to honor these American building traditions—from the faded picket fence of a weathered clapboard cottage on the coast of Maine to the rough-hewn walls of a log cabin nestled in the Rocky Mountain countryside.

Color plays a key role in the decoration of the American country interior. Whether painted in a palette of strong, full-bodied earthy colors—moss and a deep shade of bottle green, oxblood, brick red, or sapphire blue—pale gentle tones or left in their natural state, these woods—which also originally provided the main source of fuel—furnish the backdrop for a lively array of colorful decorative objects reflecting the folk art traditions brought from the home countries, such as the practice of

LEFT In a breakfast room on Long Island the walls are covered with old pine paneling. The chairs are 19th-century slat-back or ladderbacks, and the hutch is 18th-century English oak. The ceramics are also imported into the U.S.: the porcelain on the hutch from China and the tureen and ladle were made by Staffordshire potters to appeal to the American market, with a print of the Boston State House. American country style tends to be a happy mix of imports from the rest of the world with indigenous pieces.

OPPOSITE This lodge in Aspen has been much influenced by the great camps in the Adirondacks. The decorative elements on the fireplace are achieved by the use of wood retaining its bark and the geometric and carefully considered placement of twigs. The effect is further enhanced by the photographs of Native Americans by Edward S. Curtis, on the mantle, "the Atsina War Group" 1908 and, under the antler light fitting, "Renegade-type Apache" 1903. The rocker, covered in cowhide, is American Arts and Crafts.

stenciling favored by the Pennsylvania Dutch, richly patterned textiles, handmade patchwork quilts, colorful pottery, as well as the timeworn painted ladderback chairs, cupboards, tables, and hutches that were carefully placed around a room. Brought together these features can be used to decorative effect and succeed in creating the warm and comforting atmosphere that is the hallmark of the country-house style.

Comfort is fundamental to the style of country, and the numerous variations of the American colonial tradition are at home in a modern interior. One does not necessarily have to live in a clapboard Cape Cod cottage on the coast of New England to adapt the conventions that originated in the rural English countryside, such as pale subdued colors—buff, cream, and gray green—and the simple pieces of furniture—chests, tables, and the familiar Windsor chair. Nor does one have to live in the hot climate of the American South to enjoy the langorous style of the plantation house. Here spacious rooms opening out onto a veranda boast sleek floors and walls painted in cooling shades of bright white, ice blue, pale yellow, or peppermint green, which are furnished in humble versions of Georgian designs by Chippendale and Hepplewhite, which mingle happily with the plain, straightforward American pieces—including the indigenous rocking chair—that were made by local craftsmen.

The rustic log-cabin Adirondack style, which developed in the 19th century as part of a back-to-nature movement, continues in this century as a source of inspiration for the cozy comfort and relaxation of the country—the rustic rough-hewn and woven furniture constructed from a variety of woods by local artisans, wooden ceiling beams, and large stone fireplaces together sum up the idea of a refuge that is symbolic of the country philosophy. And for those with a taste for the minimal and ascetic, the modest interiors of the religious communities— the Shakers, the Quakers, and the Amish—will most certainly appeal, with rooms sparsely furnished with practical built-in cupboards and beds, and ladderback chairs.

Like the melting pot that is America itself, there is no single American country style, and elements from each of these different strands of the pastoral American tradition can be artfully combined to create a satisfying country ambience for a city townhouse, a modern high-rise apartment, a cabin in the woods, or a rural farmhouse. In the 21st century something for everyone with a taste for country style can be found in the distinctive heritage borne of the simple values, hard work, and imagination of America's first settlers.

LEFT The Captain Daniel Lord house, built in 1735, has retained the original floor plan. The kitchen at the back of the house was flanked by two smaller rooms, one the "'borning" room (for childbirth or for the sick or aged) and the other a buttery for food storage. The wide plank walls are original to the house, the sink and stone counter are based on English homes of the period. The massive pine table is where food was prepared and then eaten.

BELOW Itinerant painters used to travel round the New World with earth pigments to mix with casein and milk paint and natural plant dyes to bring color into the home. While some walls can be kept neutral, the barn red, light and dark blue, warm yellow, and a blue-green help to bring warmth.

Key to this iconic and spirited sensibility, along with a respectful appreciation of all that had come before, lay the ability and confidence to embrace the unfamiliar yet interesting, to marry the past with the future, to look for comfort—as the early settlers certainly did—in age-old traditions while exploring all that was possible, exciting, and new.

In America, the country ideal took many forms and was shaped by the heritage of the past while looking ahead to the future—a hallmark of the American spirit. Today in the 21st century the refuge from the pressures and anxieties brought about by urban life often tends to look ahead by celebrating an illustrious past that was by necessity characterized at the time by what was simple, clean-lined, and unadorned with ornament, and which was reinterpreted centuries later as sleek, chic, and quintessentially modern. The spirit of the country lifestyle that was initially brought to this new land by immigrants in the 17th century captured the imagination across America from the beginning, and these ideals continue to resonate today in a variety of states that reflect the diversity and highly original character of the country itself. The warm and cozy sanctuary typical of the country sensibility is equally at home in a 19th-century New York apartment, a seaside retreat in Maine, in the Chicago suburban houses inspired by Frank Lloyd Wright, a mountain retreat in the mountains of Colorado, or a sun-baked refuge nestled in the countryside of New Mexico. Like the ideals that define America as a nation, the interpretation of what is country remains forever modern and forward-looking. From Palm Beach to Seattle, the country aesthetic looks for inspiration to the surrounding landscape, with the clean-lined, sumptuous Art Deco designs typical of 1930s' architectural interiors reflected in a modern apartment in Los Angeles, or a farmhouse in upstate New York nestled in woodland that is sparsely furnished and revels in native materials such as wood and stone.

RIGHT Much of the woodwork in this 1827 farmhouse in Kent, Connecticut, had been stripped out. This wall was created to mimic 19th-century field paneling. The inspiration for the color, however, has come from the tones of the Connecticut fieldstone rather than historic research. The chairs are quite local—they are the Hudson Valley school circa 1880–90.

OPPOSITE This dining room in a 1730s' Connecticut Colonial house has the original hand-hewn wide floorboards. The furniture is a comfortable mix of furniture and furnishings from many countries. The oak table was made in England in the 18th century, the chair on the left is a circa 1900 copy of an American Boston "Flemish" side chair, the chair on the right is Spanish baroque, again a copy made in the 1920s. The paintings are 17th-century Italian. Most of the ceramics are Delft.

north africa

Of all the remote lands around the world that can fire the imagination and offer a dramatic and inspiring refuge for a distinctly vibrant interpretation of country style, it is the countries of North Africa—Morocco, Tunisia, and Egypt, and by extension and influence the southern reaches of the Spanish mainland—which stand proud.

ABOVE The massive mud walls of North Africa seem to have been there since time began. Tigmi Tagadert has been converted from various village houses, which are built in the local style. These high walls protect the interior courtyards from the searing desert heat.

RIGHT There is no mistaking the North African location of this hallway with the pierced wooden fretwork screen, the polychrome tiles, and reclaimed double doors. The colored glass panels and screens, in similar style, can be purchased in the local souk.

OPPOSITE In one of the guest bedrooms in Tigmi Tagadert the simple walls are kept off-white; the color is added by traditional red Berber rugs and local fabrics, woven on the premises. The ceilings are eucalyptus, and the doors and window shutters come from local houses that have been modernized.

ABOVE This palette is for the bold. Vivid reds, dazzling blues, brilliant greens, and glorious yellows—all the colors of the souk.

From the sizzling hot sultry climate to the parched scorching desert that is punctuated by a host of mosques, palaces, and gardens, the allure of the North African landscape lies in its seeming detachment from the real world, thereby making it the ideal place for seeking comfort and relaxation. Today the surrounding countryside, age-old local customs, and building traditions continue to inform the construction of a country dwelling that looks for its very foundation to the earth. The rough, uneven walls of a villa in Morocco, for example, might be constructed from local clay and plastered, while ceiling beams, narrow doors and small window openings built of local wood

keep the intense heat outside at bay. Tin-glazed terracotta tiles pave the floors of a room in a subdued checkerboard pattern or line the wainscoting, which is decoratively dressed with stylized Islamic geometric and floral motifs rendered in bright hues.

The colors and materials of the earth also play an important role in the style of North African country. The rich earth-baked reddish-brown of terracotta has for centuries featured in the hottest regions across the globe—from pots randomly scattered around a terrace to the sun-baked roof tiles that provide shelter from the blistering sun. Against a backdrop of walls painted cool white, taupe, or blue-gray to offer relief from the temperatures

arches, squares, and trefoils, for instance—and the wrought-iron grilles and pierced shutters that keep interiors private and cool are decorative as well as highly functional.

Many of these indigenous North African customs of decoration—tin-glazed terracotta tiles, wrought-iron grilles for windows, wooden doors punctuated with metal studs—coupled with a taste for the dry warm shades of the earth including sun-baked brick red, vermilion, saffron, and ocher along with cool clean colors such as sky blue, off-white, and sage green continue to resonate as symbols of the surrounding countryside. Migrating with the Moors across the Mediterranean to the European continent, these decorative traditions were enthusiastically embraced especially by southern Spain—which continues to honor this decorative tradition to this day—eventually filtering down to the New World, as seen in a hacienda located in Santa Fe or a modern apartment in the sun-baked Arizona desert.

ABOVE AND RIGHT BELOW In the midst of the bustling Medina in Marrakech, down hidden alleyways, the courtyard of a riyad is open to the skies. Everywhere in North Africa you find these pillars with shaped arches and metalwork balconies. The colors are those of the peacock, the vibrant blues and greens.

RIGHT ABOVE Riyad Edward is in the northern part of the medina of Marrakech. The inner courtyard is central to the house with all rooms radiating from it, darkened by wooden screens and grilles. In Morocco the courtyard is the oasis in the city, with the pool, the greenery, and the shade.

OPPOSITE The kitchen of Agnes Amery's riyad is open to the skies. The sand from the desert often blows in, and torrential rain storms can cause the storm drains to overflow. Tiles are the most practical and beautiful solution. The flat gray paint of the cupboards, with small carved ribbon detail, connects the floor to the walls.

outside, the vivid shades of terracotta, bright orange, golden yellow, and rich blue that are found in the traditional woven Berber textiles and carpets add a splash of color.

The age-old custom of using tin-glazed terracotta tiles for building and decorating is fundamental to the creation of a 21st-century country dwelling that draws inspiration from the decorative traditions found in the villas of Morocco and Tunisia. Nowhere is this more apparent than in the characteristic architectural feature of the inner courtyard where one escapes to find a cooling refuge from the harsh rays of the sun. Rooms traditionally lead off the central courtyard, which more often than not is open to the sky and holds pride of place as the ultimate secret hideaway. Against a backdrop of plaster walls, horseshoe-shaped arches, and balconies that have been painted in cool tranquil colors—cream, sage green, or peacock blue—floors and walls centered around a pool are faced with glossy terracotta tiles that tend to reflect the same calming shades and traditional Islamic ornamental patterns. Adding to the peaceful and cooling atmosphere are generous sofas and chairs and sumptuous plants such as bougainvillea and lemon trees.

For the modern interior the architectural simplicity of a traditional North African villa—which looks primarily to color married with practical solutions that also are ornamental—offers enormous appeal. For instance, in addition to colorful glazed tiles for floors and walls, the use of wooden, louvered, or beaded screens, massive studded wooden doors, and window frames rendered in traditional geometric shapes and patterns—

room by
room

Rooms for living in are all about
comfort and leisure, created as a
peaceful sanctuary that looks back
to the tradition of the one-room
country home for inspiration.

relaxing

At the heart of the country philosophy lies the desire for comfort and
relaxation, as well as the need to escape from a world that tends to be fraught
with everyday pressures and stress. The country lifestyle is all about living,
with nurturing surroundings the principal ingredient. Rooms for relaxing
and living in—the mantra of those who seek refuge in the country—can be
found in a host of imaginative variations. From a sleek penthouse located
high above the streets of a bustling city center to a remote stone cottage
nestled in fertile woodland or a sun-baked rural retreat—the concept of
the country has for decades played a key role in shaping the direction
of the design and decoration of the interiors we create for living.

The idea of the modern-day reception room takes inspiration from the
age-old one-room country dwelling, where living—from cooking and eating,
sleeping and taking ease, catching up on correspondence, reading, sewing,
playing games, and engaging in conversation—traditionally took place in a

RIGHT This large, airy sitting room offers a relaxed neutral canvas, by combining pale slub tones on wheat plastered walls and bleached floorboards in their offset pattern, with loose covers in complementary tones on the chairs and sofa. The play of light and shadow upon the space, emitting from the expanse of glass on two sides of the room, gives added appeal.

LEFT Summers spent in Tarn et Garonne have inspired some of Kathryn Ireland's fabric collection such as these curtains of "Floral Batik." In the small sitting room the comfortable armchairs prove irresistible to the two terriers.

OPPOSITE Neutral colors create a calm haven in this home near Cannes in the South of France. The curtains are linen, and the thick seagrass mat partially covers the chestnut boards. The chair is by Ralph Lauren.

single large room that was centered around the all-important hearth. What especially defines the contemporary country living room is the earnest effort to be comfortable and feel very much at home above all other considerations—precious treasures and self-conscious conceits have no place in this informal and relaxed atmosphere. Furniture and artefacts in a variety of styles, of different dates, traditions, and provenance mix happily together and lend a familiar and distinctive character to the country living room.

But what feels like a comfortable, cozy, and commodious room for living and relaxing in one part of the world might be stifling and decidedly at odds in another. While those living in cold and icy regions may look to create a warm sanctuary furnished with a roaring open fire, tables, and paneling rendered in time-worn timber, generous plush sofas and chairs, and curtains

fashioned from dense, hard-wearing fabrics in jewel-like colors—by contrast steamy climates seek a cool and refreshing shelter that is defined by tiled floors, light-colored walls, ceiling fans, and windows that are shuttered or covered in the thinnest of natural fabrics such as voile, linen, or silk. However, one of the great charms of the country concept dictates that rules are made to be broken; hence it would not be unusual to find in a Scandinavian farmhouse a living room painted in a cool palette that reflects the pale tones that are found in the abundant surrounding landscape or in the sizzling heat of New Mexico or Morocco a reception room decorated in the rich, spicy shades of yellow, ocher, or deep green.

The decoration of a living room that celebrates country style need not be a theatrical pastiche that looks back to the past or to homespun rural traditions—of worn fabrics in cabbage rose patterns, spriggy floral wallpaper meandering over walls and ceilings, peeling paint on every available surface, and simple vernacular furniture made of oak or elm. The simplicity and innocence of country can also be found thriving in a more sophisticated vision that is at once bold and modern—in the cool clean lines of a table rendered in molded aluminum, a luxurious sofa covered with distressed leather, a country-style fireplace that appears at first glance to have been

CLOCKWISE FROM TOP LEFT
The main salon in this early 19th-century coaching inn in northern France has rough plaster walls and original beams painted a distressed icy green all over—the color was inspired by frost in the landscape. The two chairs on the right and the sofa were designed by the owner Julie Prisca; they are upholstered in neutral colors with a hint of lavender. The high ceilings are the distinctive feature of this home in the mountains of Norway. The comfortable sofas pick up tones from the local stone. The focus of the room is the large windows, allowing spectacular views over the valley to mountains beyond. Comfort and practicality were the main criteria when Ron Mason designed the original log house on the site overlooking the Arkansas River in Colorado. Everything is natural, from the lodge-pole pine logs from a standing dead forest in

Montana to the leather sofas and chairs, from the wrought iron stairs to the sleeping platform above.
On the same site but 20 years later Ron constructed "The Tube" with tongue-and-groove southern yellow pine walls. It is a modern-day boxcar cantilevered over the river. The screen was designed by Charles and Ray Eames, the lamp by Castiglioni, and the tables and sofa are from www.designwithinreach.com.
In the living room of an English family home, whites, a selection of different off-whites, and beige create a cool serene environment.
A converted 19th-century carriage house in upstate New York has been transformed into a neoclassical hideaway by artist Frank Faulkner. The walls are varying tones of gray, and the floors covered in sisal all serve as a backdrop for the reclaimed 19th-century French fireplace and Frank's collection of antiques.

constructed of natural stone, but which in reality has been cleverly assembled of man-made materials, a wall painted in pale cream shades that furnishes a backdrop for a colorful abstract painting, an eye-catching lamp, or ceiling beams constructed from age-old reclaimed railroad ties.

The quest for a country-style living space that has been designed for relaxation and comfort is not confined to the interior of a dwelling. Solace, renewal, and a sense of tranquillity are also achieved by reaching out to incorporate nature in the garden or on a terrace or balcony. Here outdoor "rooms" that boast a sense of light and space—having been especially created for passing hours in quiet contemplation of the surrounding plants and flowers, for appreciating the scents, smells, and sounds, for dining, for sharing time with friends and family—also play a key role in realizing the desire to leave behind the day-to-day stresses created by modern life.

ABOVE An eclectic mix of artifacts comprising simple, geometric forms offer intriguing points of focus in this urban Belgian sitting room. The architectural principles of antiquity—cube, arch, sphere, and triangle—are well represented in this room scheme. The wood floor and plaster walls steer the eye to the objects, as if in a living art gallery.

LEFT In Riyad Edward in Marrakech a small internal sitting area is the ideal place to take mint tea. The black and white tiled floors, with small minaret detailing, the ancient wooden doors, and the shaped arches are all sure signs of North African construction. The fabric and rugs are available in the souk as are the colored glass and brass lantern.

OPPOSITE One of the main criteria for relaxation in North Africa is to find a dark, cool place to escape the glare of the sun. Inspired by a 17th-century Dutch oil painting, Belgian designer Agnes Emery has used her tiles, sage green walls, and banquettes covered in lush green velvet to create a womblike haven. The large green and blue velvet cushions are decorated with birds of paradise, or *oiseux menchant*. At night this whole area is lit with hundreds of small candles, further enhancing the magic.

BELOW Sitting on locally crafted low chairs, a visitor can enjoy a refreshing cup of mint tea. This upstairs balcony, looking onto the open courtyard below, has a soothing combination of blue and gray. The tiled floor has a repeating pattern of eight tiles with stylized roses, inspired by old Iznik tiles in the local souk.

LEFT For guests at Riyad Edward, relaxation can be found by the central pool or in the shade of the covered terrace. Elaborate wooden screens and grilles protect the open windows into the dining room.

ABOVE In the center of the vineyard a charming grouping of a simple round table, a bench, and wooden chairs are shaded by overhanging trees—a perfect natural arbour.

LEFT Refreshments can be served on the back deck of this cabin overlooking Oslo fjord. This area is quite protected, as the wind tends to come from the south. In June the area in front of the deck is covered with wildflowers. The blue of the chair cushions and the plant troughs echo the expanse of water.

BELOW On the terrace of Gilles Pellerin's home in the South of France, shade is provided by a simple canvas stretched between poles to resemble a sail. The old stone wall has been utilized to create a banquette, backed with fragrant plants and made more comfortable by linen-covered cushions.

Today the fundamental charm
and appeal of rooms designed for
cooking and eating looks back to the
traditional role of the country kitchen
as the heart of the household, where
family and friends gathered to share a
meal, to work, and to relax.

cooking
and eating

OPPOSITE The kitchen of this wooden lodge in Norway has a fresh natural look. The simple white cabinets and painted tongue-and-groove ceiling, the linen blind at the window and exposed floorboards all provide a restful family eating area. A set of Windsor chairs surrounds a massive oak pedestal table.

BELOW The kitchen in this Normandy coaching inn is a comfortable mix of old and new. The floor is painted concrete, partially covered with old Kazak rugs. This is the center of the home, with the new table surrounded by old painted chairs in front of the covered combined stove and fire.

From the sunny warmth of Italy to the frostbitten climate of Scandinavia, a pivotal ingredient and one of the highlights of the country house surely must be the space that throughout history has been given over to areas for the pleasurable pastimes of cooking and eating. By definition the country house offers refuge and comfort from the everyday pressures of modern life. So it is only natural that the kitchen—which for centuries has enjoyed its pivotal role as the hub of the home and by extension any other rooms designated for dining—should take pride of place as the heart of the household, where families come together to be nourished, to work, and to relax. Both the pulse and wellspring of contentment, the country kitchen manages to accommodate the tools of contemporary life, while at the same time embracing and reinterpreting the colorful lifestyle of the rural past.

Traditionally country homes have boasted a dining room that played a key role as part of a multipurpose kitchen alongside a living space. In the 18th century, England forged a path as the first European country to create a room specifically for eating. But although the fashionable nobility enjoyed

dining in this new and highly stylish spectacle, the kitchen remained, well into the 19th century, the primary center for eating and family activity among the majority of the population. In both Europe and across the Atlantic, the burgeoning middle classes developed a taste for easy and pleasant dining rooms, which tended to be furnished with an amalgam of rustic and contemporary decorative objects alongside 18th-century antiques.

The aesthetic that defines the country experience today is very much one of comfort and security as well as of freedom and leisure. There exists no better insulation from the outside world than the hospitable, and intimate atmosphere that has been created with spaces designated for cooking and eating—for joyous celebrations, where family and friends gather to unwind, and share laughter, good food lovingly prepared, and easy conversation. For

ABOVE This Normandy kitchen was remodeled by fabric designer Dominique Kieffer. The old pine *atelier* table was found in a Paris flea market. The chairs are re-editions of a 1930's design with cushions covered with Dominique's "Unis" cotton. The appliances are all brushed steel—very hi-tech, in contrast to the Creil faience plates on the wall, from the "Monuments de Paris" series 1810.

OPPOSITE In the massive kitchen of a stone farmhouse built circa 1820 near St. Rémy in France, the designer Jean Louis Reynaud has created the perfect heart of the home around the original fireplace. He designed the table and found the perfect early 20th-century American Arts and Crafts chairs.

CLOCKWISE FROM TOP LEFT
In a Dutch vineyard, a timeless large pine farmhouse table and chairs provide the ideal dining area. They sit on a worn terracotta floor and under a ceiling of painted beams.
In Marrakech lunch in the shade is a local tagine of lamb and dates. The pale natural ocher paint of the walls is punctuated by the decorative window grille. In the evening, light is provided by numerous Moroccan lanterns bought in the local souk.
A feeling of simplicity and coolness is paramount in this adobe-style kitchen near Santa Fe. The white units, with aluminum surfaces and appliances are supremely functional, as is the square-edged wooden integrated breakfast banquette.
Tiles are an extremely practical solution for kitchens, particularly when the kitchen is partly open to the elements, as here in Marrakech.

Designer Agnes Emery has designed the tiles herself in shades of blue and gray with many patterns, some inspired by Renaissance tiles.
In this elegant kitchen in upstate New York, Frank Faulkner has used the old pine bead boards salvaged from the original 1880s carriage house to create his kitchen cabinets. The work surface is soapstone. To give another color accent, the backsplash is rich deep brown.
The La Cornue stove is at the heart of this kitchen in the L'Orangerie in the hills above Cannes. Old local stone is used to decorative effect on the end wall and modern ironwork, used in traditional style, provides decorative grilles. The units are painted in shades of taupe.

some, cooking is itself a relaxing pastime, a way to reconnect not only with kith and kin, but also with the land. For others it is the satisfaction of the experience of getting together to enjoy cooking and eating that makes the kitchen and the dining room the most beloved of rooms in a cutting-edge modern 21st-century apartment in Paris, a colorful hacienda nestled in the sunburned landscape of Albuquerque, or in a traditional Swedish farmhouse hidden in the countryside far away from the bustle of Stockholm.

In today's world, the dining room of a home inspired by the countryside ideology looks to create an easy and calm setting that echoes the farmhouse kitchen. Against this backdrop furniture tends to be simple, with a sturdy pine table surrounded by homey, rush-seated chairs constructed in a variety of woods and country styles—from Windsor and ladderback, cupboards in pine, oak, and elm, faded fabrics, and modest pottery tableware—that echo the warmth of the rural lifestyle. Yet the desire for country simplicity can also be found in an uncluttered minimalist kitchen and dining space—with sleek modern appliances, clean-lined tables and chairs rendered in natural materials including leather and oak, or man-made materials such as brushed aluminum and Lucite. Mediterranean countries embrace nature with outdoor rooms for dining on stone or tiled terraces, while a New England cottage or a Swedish farmhouse keep the cold weather at bay with an open fireplace.

BELOW In vineyards everywhere there is a tradition of workers sitting together around an enormous table in the open air, relaxing and eating after a strenuous day in the fields. Peter de Wit's vineyard, Domaine d'Heerstaayen in the south of Holland, is no exception.

BOTTOM The sponged ocher walls with floral stenciled decoration make a sunny breakfast area. The old oak low hutch, pine table, and country chairs add to a light modern feel with a traditional twist.

RIGHT These sponged plaster walls with soft off-white lend a monastic feel to this minimalist interior. The simple low Chinese chairs, of centuries-old design, add to the overall serenity of this dining area.

Bedrooms and bathrooms furnish the ultimate escape from the world, as private and intimate spaces designed to refresh, rejuvenate, and renew.

sleeping and bathing

OPPOSITE Frank Faulkner has created the perfect classical country bedroom. In his strict black, white, and gray scheme, even the wood of his four-poster, bought from Bloomingdales in 1983, is painted white .

BELOW In Michael Leva's Connecticut home the master bedroom has a bed with Shakerlike simplicity. The simple wooden structure has been painted, as have the pair of Louis Philippe country armchairs.

For those who embrace country living, the importance placed upon comfort and the need for a relaxing retreat, far removed from the hectic pace of modern life, plays a pivotal role in the decoration of rooms for living—be it a warm and snug kitchen centered at the heart of the house, a commodious living room for enjoying quiet pastimes such as reading or entertaining friends, or a sheltering garden terrace surrounded by honeysuckle and jasmine. The creation of a nurturing environment as an escape from day-to-day pressures forms an essential component of the country house aesthetic. And nowhere can be found a more evocative interpretation of this philosophy than in rooms that have been designed for sleeping and bathing.

By definition, bedrooms and bathrooms are intimate spaces that celebrate the concept of refuge and retreat in a totally personal way. Whether it is a sophisticated cutting-edge modern apartment in the heart of bustling Rome that has been decorated in a minimal style with an imaginative combination of steel and glass, a homey "shabby-chic" cottage nestled within the lush and picturesque foothills of the French countryside whose character relies upon

LEFT In a Normandy manor house a pair of 19th-century metal campaign beds are softened by natural fabrics and colors. The 19th-century German chairs were heavy carved mahogany with dark leather upholstery. They were given a totally new look—they were painted white, and the leather was covered with tied linen covers.

RIGHT In keeping with the rustic simplicity of this Taos retreat, Alexandra Champalimaud's simply constructed four-poster is draped in natural linens. The bed mirrors the chinked construction of the walls.

faded fabrics and battered wooden floors, or a cool villa rendered in stone in the southern reaches of Spain that inside boasts an array of vibrant colors that look to the surrounding landscape for inspiration—all share in common rooms that have been created for individual needs and private indulgences, including ablutions and catching up on sleep.

Until the Middle Ages, separate rooms for sleeping existed only in very grand houses, as one large reception room usually furnished a family with space for eating, cooking, and sleeping communally, and it was not until the 18th century that private bedrooms became commonplace.

Rooms designated for sleeping tend, by their very function, to be exclusive and highly personal spaces, so their decoration frequently may also be inspired retreats that reflect fantasy alongside what is both functional and practical. Romantic ideals—faded floral fabrics, wallpapers boasting delicate patterns, antique poster beds, colorful rugs, and favourite trinkets that lend a

LEFT Dramatic navy blue printed toile with simple complementary blue-and-white gingham brighten up a children's bedroom in Kathryn Ireland's home in the South of France.

touch of whimsy and help to create a cozy atmosphere—happily marry with modern appliances such as sophisticated audio-visual systems, while timeworn natural wood and stone may be complemented by hard-edged contemporary materials such as brushed steel that are softened by plain linens and cottons in cool pale shades of cream and gray. A taste for the exotic—vibrant shades of persimmon and vivid greens both calm and excite the senses, treasured collectibles that hold memories of long-ago travels, and the simple, streamlined geometric shapes typically found in China, Japan, and the Near East—frequently finds voice within traditional surroundings, lending rooms dedicated to what is intimate and highly personal the perfect expression of individual taste and unfettered imagination.

Rooms set aside for sleeping are essentially hideaway spaces dedicated to preparations, both physical and mental, for greeting the day and for the rituals and customs for unwinding and recharging at night. Natural fabrics, paint, and wallpaper in both modern and traditional interiors tend to be either cool and restful in pale shades, including white, straw, celery, sky blue, and lilac, for example, or in warm and cozy jewellike tones such as sapphire, emerald or ruby. Comfortable and supportive mattresses, crisp cotton or linen sheets, plenty of plump pillows, decorative coverlets, and favorite ornaments and bibelots add to the relaxed and intimate atmosphere.

ABOVE LEFT In an 18th-century Connecticut colonial home, old 18th-century French toile bed hangings drape an 1830 Pennsylvania four-poster bed.

LEFT The furniture is original to this Norwegian cabin built in 1925. In a naturally dark interior it was important to paint the furniture white and use various blue-and-white fabrics to add pattern and texture.

OPPOSITE, CLOCKWISE FROM LEFT
The master bedroom of Gilles Pellerin's house makes full use of the spectacular views over the gardens to the Bay of Cannes in the distance. The colors are neutral, white to beige, with texture added with suedes, cashmeres, and linens.
The wooden walls of this Norwegian lodge in the mountains are painted cream with a light burnt umber streaked effect. Wood is also used as a decorative effect on the oversized bed headboard.
Two takes on a Moroccan bedroom: the first in Riyad Edward is light, airy, almost monastic in its décor; the second uses decorative patterned tiles and luxuriant color.

ABOVE In the master bedroom of this Adirondack-inspired lodge in Aspen, the bed has been constructed from large branches and twigs from fallen trees found on the property. The bedspread and cushions are made from Hungarian felted wool.

ABOVE RIGHT The guest bedroom in this stone Federal house in Connecticut has, in addition to the wall of Connecticut fieldstone, three rough-hewn limed plank walls. The eight framed "herbiers", pressed herb-and-flower pictures, bring the garden into the bedroom.

RIGHT The sleeping loft in the guest cabin was designed by Ron Mason, with its window wall, to make full use of the spectacular views of the Arkansas River and the "Fourteeners", five mountains in this part of the Rockies over 14,000ft (4,265m).

OPPOSITE Exposing the original wooden structure in this Belgian house imparts a rustic charm. Painting the beams and walls with an overall off-white unifies the scheme.

bathing
With a brief tradition that looks back only to the late 19th century, rooms specially designed for bathing have not always enjoyed the pride of place they now do in our homes. While the fixtures have been around for a long time—large ceramic bathtubs dating back as far as 4000B.C. have been found in Crete—bathing continued to be a communal activity, carried out in public bathhouses, for many centuries. It was only with the invention of modern heating and plumbing systems, and the introduction of hot and cold water ducted freely around the home, that the bathroom became the private and personal sanctuary we are familiar with.

Whether clean-lined, spare and modern or reflecting indigenous traditions, bathrooms furnish the *ne plus ultra* experience for pleasure and relaxation. In addition to being practical, these spaces frequently enjoy broad strokes of originality and a creative spirit however restrained and uncontrived—sweeping expanses of window glass that bring the outside in for quiet contemplation, mirrors to enlarge the interior space, and colors and materials that have been taken from the surrounding landscape.

Bedrooms and bathrooms are the ultimate retreats for comfort and relaxation, hidden away from the stresses imposed by the modern world. But despite the highly personal nature of these spaces there are also those additional rooms that have been created and decorated as welcoming and hospitable sanctuaries for visiting family and friends, the guest bedrooms and bathrooms. Thus the intimate refuge of bed and bath can also be made to extend a warm greeting and to offer a temporary refuge from the world.

OPPOSITE The walls of this bathroom overlooking Cannes are finished in the traditional Moroccan tadelakt render technique. A special lime render is applied and compressed with stones, which results in a compact shiny surface. The color tone of the tadelakt is not regular, as in normal pigmented render, but depends on the application. Where the material is a bit more compressed, a darker color tone will result. The surface of the tadelakt seems to change in color tones depending on light conditions. With the natural exposed boards and sunken bath, the attention is focused outside, to the beautiful gardens and the bay of Cannes.

ABOVE This private bathroom in Normandy has a pleasing beige and dark flat gray scheme. The washbasin was originally in a school.

BELOW In Norway, tongue-and-groove wooden paneling is painted off-white, contrasting with the dark tones of the frames. All the handles are made from dark leather.

ABOVE LEFT The formal Renaissance-inspired floor tiles in this Moroccan bathroom contrast with the more natural wall tiles, which have a dappled effect. The overall atmosphere of the room is light and airy.

ABOVE CENTER Again in Morocco, the shower is concealed in a traditionally shaped *hammam*, or steam room. The walls are covered with tadelakt, which is naturally water resistant.

ABOVE RIGHT Traditional bathroom fixtures and accessories, both original and contemporary, are now available from a large number of suppliers. Here in Holland, the classical simplicity is enhanced by the floor covering of black-and-white tiles.

RIGHT In Normandy, an original 19th-century rolltop bathtub is painted dark gray. The tongue-and-groove walls and full-height closet doors are painted palest lilac.

ABOVE LEFT Tadelakt is the wall finish again, but this time in the South of France. The basins are limestone with storage baskets set on a chestnut shelf beneath.

ABOVE CENTER The warmth of this bathroom in Colorado comes from the walls of Southern yellow pine. There is no need for added decoration, just the window with views of the Rockies and the ample white bath by Duravit and taps by Axor.

ABOVE RIGHT In Pennsylvania this shower room is made from Corian. It was moulded off-site and finished on-site. As a wet room it is ideal as Corian is completely waterproof. The wash hand basin is by Catalano.

LEFT In the adobe-style house near Santa Fe the walls of the guest bathroom are unfinished concrete. They provide a very natural backdrop to the ultra modern bath. The window looks out to the outdoor shower.

structural features

Central to defining an authentic country-style interior lies the treatment of structural features such as walls, where the atmosphere of comfort and relaxation depends upon a backdrop of colors and textures to create a warm and inviting refuge from the outside world.

walls

LEFT In Morocco, mud walls have been constructed for centuries. The village houses in hamlets such as Tagadert are still built using sand, small stones, and straw. They tend to have an organic quality, with door openings, windows, and niches punched into the solid walls.

BELOW The walls of this small "office" are painted with chalk and natural pigment (painted using the earth found on the property itself). The curved chair is a Chinese Ming-period chair, from which the lacquer has almost disappeared.

OPPOSITE LEFT A simple narrow tongue-and-groove wall painted pale pink with a painted Shaker-style pegboard and a painted French late 19th-century bed in the Cotswold in England brings a little touch of France to a house.

OPPOSITE RIGHT The plaster walls in this hunting lodge in the Périgord region of France have been color washed in subtle tones of ocher and yellow. Colorwashes give a softer timeless look; flat colors can look modern and harsh in a period room.

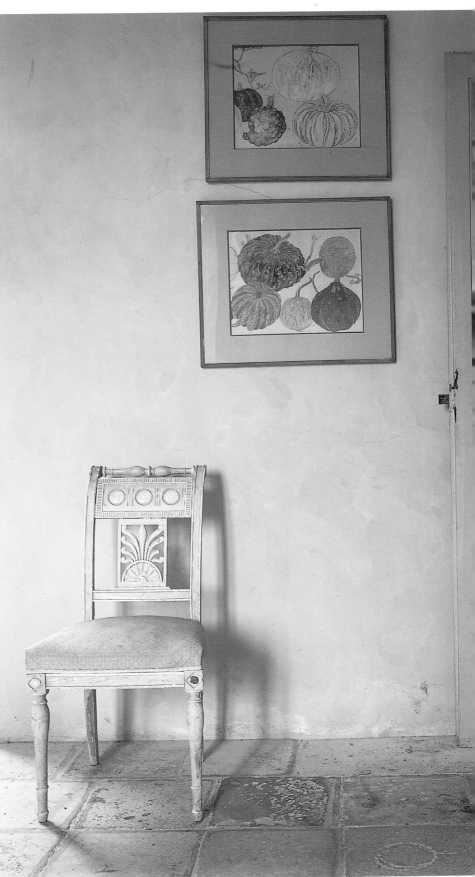

From the scorched earth and hot, sultry temperatures of New Mexico and Morocco to the cold and frosty climates typical of Scandinavia and Colorado—the decoration of a country-style dwelling looks for inspiration to the surrounding landscape. The use of raw natural materials for building—wood, brick, and stone, for example—bring the flavor of the outside into the rooms of a cozy thatch-roofed cottage nestled in England's Cotswolds, a spacious sun-baked villa in Sicily, or a clean-lined modern apartment in the heart of Paris or New York, as does a color palette influenced by steel and glass or the indigenous flora and fauna dotted across the local countryside. Colors and textures commingle to weave a highly original and imaginative interior that forges a powerful connection with the land.

The internal walls of a country dwelling may embrace a variety of surfaces—wood, cob, plaster, rough uneven stone, untreated or painted brick—which generally are determined by available local materials and building customs. In England a cob house, for example, traditionally boasts walls that have been filled with a composite of clay subsoil and chopped straw, while a log cabin or farmhouse located in Scandinavia or rural America and decorated with an eye to the countryside—areas typically surrounded by forests—tend to feature wood-paneled walls that are shaded with a timeworn, mellow patina.

The charm and appeal that lies at the heart of country style owes a great deal—in concert with ceilings and floors—to the relatively rough and uncomplicated character of the walls. Lime-washed walls constructed of brick or stone, rough plasterwork

OPPOSITE Deep colors painted onto the walls and ceiling pick up the tones in the floor tiles. The effect is womblike. The richness of the colors in this bedroom in a riyad in Marrakech echoes the abundant colors to be found in the local souk.

RIGHT The solid gray color of the walls in a Normandy manor house bedroom throws into sharp focus the plaster medallions and artwork. The metal bed is a copy of a 19th-century frame. It is covered with an antique French *boutis*, or quilt.

BELOW The stairs and walls leading from the kitchen to the upstairs rooms of this 18th-century Connecticut colonial home are painted a traditional barn red.

enhanced by exposed ceiling beams, walls made up of chinked wood or tongue-and-groove paneling or constructed of oak or pine that incorporate cupboards and have been waxed to a rich hue, painted in pale colors or rich earth tones or covered with the distressed woodwork that points to the passage of time—these number among the distinctive features that at once highlight the unpretentious and practical nature of rural traditions, which ultimately define the style of a country interior.

The treatment of walls often can be closely linked with the underlying architectural structure. A feature such as a fireplace surround that has been incorporated into a wall plays both a utilitarian as well as a decorative role, while the addition of a dado painted in bright colors or pale shades adds proportion to a high-ceilinged room as well as making a decorative statement. Ornamental conceits might also be linked to the principal function of a room—shimmering, brightly colored ceramic tiles made by local craftsmen are at home when lining the walls of a bathroom, whereas a glance back to a 17th-century Netherlandish tradition may find handpainted faience tiles artfully displayed around a kitchen sink.

The treatment of walls for a country-style interior might take a lead from a practice that reaches back to medieval times, when it was common for the wealthy to cover their walls with silk tapestries and wall hangings in vibrant hues, although those living in more humble country dwellings relied for decoration on painted cloths made of canvas or linen. Still another wall treatment that continues to find favor looks to the 18th century for inspiration, when papering walls with flock paper in

imitation of more expensive tapestry, silk, or damask textile wall hangings became fashionable. The manufacture of wallpapers featuring designs covering a wide range of subjects, from flower sprays and plants, birds, landscapes, and colorful figural scenes has made it possible to decorate a room more cheaply, to cover flaws in the woodwork, and to add cozy warmth to the interior. The practice of using paper to simulate wall paneling and architectural moldings and plasterwork to cover walls—made popular in the 19th century by the company of William Morris, among others—affords another practical and inexpensive method for creating a warm and comfortable atmosphere.

Other touches include pasting prints and engravings directly onto walls, painting the entire surface of a wall in a single pale shade that matches the color of the ceiling, then embellished with a handpainted frieze, hung with wallpapers patterned with stencil designs adapted from the flora and fauna of rural life, or embracing the practice—rooted in the fresco paintings of classical antiquity as well as in folk traditions—of painting directly onto walls with landscapes scenes of flowers, fruit, and trees that bring the delights of the garden into the interior.

ABOVE The main bathroom in this wooden lodge in Aspen is dominated by the massive chinked logs. In this modern adaptation of an ancient technique, the chinking is polymer, to allow for shrinkage. The standing dead logs from Montana retain some of their bark, which becomes a decorative feature. The shower room walls are made from local stone.

OPPOSITE "The Tube", designed by Ron Mason as the living area in his settlement in Colorado, is encased with horizontal tongue-and-groove southern yellow pine walls.

RIGHT The walls of this sitting area in a Norwegian cabin are lined with wide stained pine boards.

Color is the key ingredient for the creation of a warm and comfortable country-style retreat. The color palette found in the surrounding landscape, which is extensive and brimming with variety, dictates the colors adopted for decorating the walls of a country-style interior. The terracottas, brick reds, browns, and moss greens of the earth evoke the natural dyes and pigments that were favored in the 18th century in the American Colonial interior and which remain especially well matched to country-style furniture. In areas that enjoy hot weather all year round—North Africa, Spain, and New Mexico to name a few—it is bright white along with pale dry shades—light terracottas, buffs, and soft yellows that reflect the warm sand and dust of the arid desert—that proffer a welcome and refreshing refuge from the sizzling heat by tempering the intense and vivid tones of the surrounding landscape—bright green, fiery vermilion. Rich, jewel-bright colors—emerald and sapphire blue—hold pride of place on the walls of a Mediterranean villa, while in the frosty cold climate of Scandinavia pale timeworn colors of clotted cream and vanilla punctuated by the soft shades mirrored in the local flora—leaf greens and washed browns along with

the pale pink of roses and the pale blue of harebells—impose calm and extend daylight, while the use of deep rich hues brings warmth and holds at bay the chill of the outside world.

Whatever the color, it is how the paint has been handled—the quick thick strokes laid on in a cursory fashion, the insouciant attitude to layers of paint and the swelling surfaces—which lend them a genuine country look. Techniques such as colorwashing or the addition of limewash to pigments add even to new plasterwork the appearance of soft weathering by both time and sun. The gentle colors of milk paint—traditionally applied as a flat coat for everything from walls to furniture—possess the mellow beauty brought about by the passing years. An especially effective method for achieving the soft and luminous country look is achieved by combining various shades of one color—such as yellow or terracotta—and coating different sections of walls with these assorted hues.

Whether cool and pale or bright and warm, color on walls plays a pivotal role in bringing a cosy and comfortable mood to the rooms of an interior decorated in country style, celebrating the charms of rural living while creating a welcome retreat.

ABOVE LEFT The rich blue pigment on the upper part of the walls was mixed by Agnes Emery especially for her Moroccan house. As the central courtyard is open, the walls seem to merge with the blue of the skies.

ABOVE RIGHT Many of Agnes Emery's tiles have been inspired by the tiles, old and new, she discovered in the souk. She uses many subtly different patterns while retaining the blue/green/gray theme. The mirrored tiles form a frame around the gray painted door and reflect the lemon trees in the courtyard beyond.

OPPOSITE The modulating tones of green create a fish-scale effect in the small downstairs washroom. The brass stag faucet is another of Agnes Emery's designs.

LEFT The terracotta tiles are the ideal flooring for a large country kitchen. The varying color is the natural consequence of where they were placed in the kiln.

BELOW Black and white tiled floors have been popular since Roman times. Historically, the use of ceramic floor tiles goes back to the 4th millennium B.C., in the Near and Far East.

OPPOSITE ABOVE The floor in this early 19th-century farmhouse in Provence is reclaimed 18th-century limestone flagstones, with their characteristic muted colors.

OPPOSITE BELOW The old flagstones in this 18th-century house in the Cotswolds were quarried locally.

floors

Since the Middle Ages, when they were chiefly composed of beaten earth scattered with rushes and straw that was easily swept clean, floors have gradually evolved over the centuries to embrace a wide variety of materials that play a key role in bringing to a room a flavor of the country.

Like the architectural framework of a country dwelling, the composition of the floors will largely depend upon the kinds of materials that are locally available and will naturally differ from one part of the world to another. From the colorful countryside of southern France to the New England coast, in the isolated provinces of Sweden and the sun-baked terrain of North Africa, floors can be found in a broad range of materials that speak of nothing so much as their indigenous country style.

Even a single country might share several different types of flooring according to region. For example in southern and eastern England, bricks, pammets—which were the East Anglian interpretation of French Provençal tiles that resemble terracotta squares—and quarry tiles are favored, while the floors of houses located in the north, central, and western areas of the country tend to be laid with flagstones. While Provence shares with Italy and Spain the taste for terracotta tiles that reflects the warmth abd abundance of the landscape, other parts of France usually feature tile floors colored in black and white.

By contrast, the country-style houses found in timber-rich Scandinavia and across much of North America generally rely upon the surrounding forests to create wooden floors that also bring an element of the outside in. In Scandinavia wooden floors are painted in different shades or scrubbed—traditionally they were cleaned or scoured by vigorously rubbing a wet paste of sand into the planks, which the passing of time bleached to a pale flat shade—and topped with long, narrow handwoven

runners in high-traffic areas. Houses in America commonly boast hardwood floors that are allowed to display their prized grain and markings—they have been polished to a high shine to enhance their natural beauty, and laid with colorful hooked or woven rugs, rush matting, canvas floorcloths painted with simple patterns, or stenciled with simple geometric designs.

Just as the design of walls, ceilings, doors, and staircases have the potential to create the comfortable and relaxing ambience that lies at the heart of country style, so also can floors work to create the same kind of magic. A country-style floor—whether in a high-rise contemporary kitchen or across the hearth of a stone cottage—when not laid too perfectly

celebrates the odd flaw and occasional irregularity that creates an atmosphere of considerable charm and originality. The dips and grooves worn into brick floors that evoke the passage of time, colored and textured terracotta tiles and rough-hewn stones or planks of different sizes made of oak or pine—all help in the creation of a cozy and nurturing country refuge.

The treatment of floors might also play an important role in the furnishing of a country-style interior. While an oak floor with a rich, timeworn sheen needs no further embellishment, floorboards made up of inexpensive wood such as fir or pine might be painted to disguise unsightly knotty surfaces or treated with colored stains, waxes, and varnish to resemble a more luxurious, more desirable floor finish. Pickling will create a handsome silvery patina on wood that brings a breath of clean fresh air into a room, and plain bricks or tiles that are laid in imaginative ornamental patterns add a decorative touch.

Today the continued use of time-honored local traditions testifies to the enduring appeal of country style—whether a Spanish villa boasting a pebble-floored courtyard and a kitchen floor laid with stone-chipped patterns that have been edged with brick, the medieval reliance on rush matting for covering wood planked floors that has been taken up for the rooms of a Connecticut farmhouse or the colorful hooked rugs scattered across the flagstone floors of a thatch-roofed English cottage.

ABOVE The wide mellow-toned elm floorboards are original to this mid 18th-century Connecticut house.

LEFT The floors in this Pennsylvanian house, built about 1800, are made from reclaimed pine barn sidings.

OPPOSITE The wide chestnut boards were introduced to this Provençal house when it was rebuilt four years ago using a selection of old and reclaimed materials.

LEFT These reclaimed 18th-century doors lead from the living area of Gilles Pellerin's house to the bedrooms. They have been left unpainted to display the old wood, but in the 18th century they would have been painted.

OPPOSITE, TOP LEFT TO RIGHT In Santa Fe, the early 19th-century doors leading to the guesthouse were bought in Mexico. An unusual polished latch offers a charming detail to this bleached paneled door. An old wooden studded door, bought in the souk in Marrakech, has been reused in Tigmi Tagadert.
OPPOSITE, CENTER LEFT TO RIGHT In Norway a wooden painted door with diamond pattern leads from the modern extension to the 1925 cabin.
There is no denying the heritage of this frame and door; the shapes, decoration, ancient ironwork, and color are all distinctly North African.
The exceptionally wide wooden planks of this door indicate considerable age.
OPPOSITE, BOTTOM LEFT TO RIGHT This sturdy paneled door, painted a washed denim blue, leads to a pantry with its wall-to-wall bricked inlayed floor.
Modern gray shutter doors blend with the local fieldstone in the South of France. This studded wooden door is painted in a shade of blue used traditionally in Marrakech, Essouira, and Assila in Morocco.

doors

The focal point of a domestic façade, doors are practical architectural features traditionally constructed to keep the elements at bay as well as to greet the outside world. Along with gates and gateways, the doors and doorways of country dwellings both seduce and invite while setting the tone for what will come next.

The simple honesty of materials and humble workmanship signal the rural origins of country style, and like architectural features such as floors and walls, ceilings and staircases, the construction of doors for a country dwelling inevitably depends upon reaching out to the surrounding landscape and local building traditions. In England, for example, early doors were built from interlinked planks secured with horizontal ties, until the 18th century when the paneled door—which remains fashionable today—became a practical, popular alternative.

A number of different timbers that in the past were commonly used in the creation of the doors and doorways of a country house still remain in favor in the 21st century—from the preference for hardwoods such as oak or mahogany, which tend to be found in grand country dwellings, to the more humble doors of the country cottage constructed from well-seasoned woods such as pine or fir that were usually painted to disguise unsightly flaws in the figure of the timber.

Doors for the country house enjoy a host of decorative advantages that are borne of necessity. Hardware—locks, hinges, and latches as well as doorknobs and knockers, which are also known as "door furniture"—has typically been made of cast iron or brass burnished to a high shine, incised with ornamental patterns, or occasionally dressed with a coat of paint.

OPPOSITE, TOP LEFT TO RIGHT From the front door, you get a full view of the same cantilevered staircase with original tiled floor. The second-floor staircase in this late 19th-century farmhouse has a simple wooden cantilever construction. It would originally have been painted. The kitchen in this house in upstate New York is in the stone-walled basement. This was a house of great status, and the stairway has finely turned banisters and newel posts. OPPOSITE, CENTER LEFT TO RIGHT An enclosed staircase leads to the bedrooms in this Dutch farmer's house from circa 1730 in the Hudson River Valley in New York state. The paneling and door are painted with "Salem Brick" from Old Village Paints. This simple staircase of blue tiles leads to the roof terrace in Agnes Emery's riyad in Morocco. The main stairway in this Normandy coaching inn built in 1830 is painted "Young Pine Green," mixed by Julie Prisca. OPPOSITE, BOTTOM LEFT TO RIGHT Old barn sidings were used to create the stairs in this Pennsylvania cottage. They have not been treated since the owners wanted them to age naturally. These stair treads show ample signs of age. The wooden walls show the marks of the original lathe and plaster which has been removed. In this Federal house in Connecticut, the fine architectural banisters have been painted to reflect the colors of the fieldstone walls.

RIGHT This cantilevered stairway with simple balusters is original to the manor house built in Normandy in 1830.

stairs

Essentially stairs form the structural core of a house while seeming to spring from the surrounding landscape, and in a simply furnished country dwelling they can be both an important decorative feature as well as an incredibly practical one.

There are as many variations of the staircase as there are architectural styles. In an effort to maximize space, stairs have been traditionally constructed to lead up to the next level. Native customs and lifestyle have tended to dictate the disposition and use of rooms on this next floor—additional bedrooms, storage space, or a hideaway attic, and in hot countries one tended to seek warmth by moving upstairs during colder winter months.

Whether a neat timeworn stone cottage, a spacious adobe villa, or a slick modern apartment, the construction of the staircase tends to reflect local building traditions. Twisting and turning, tucked beneath a dormer, behind a paneled cupboard door, or seemingly rising up from the center of the house—stairs inevitably make a dramatic statement. From an open string staircase that appears to be made only of treads and risers that seem to pile up in mid-air on top of each other to steps made of oak and coated with timeworn layers of beeswax or less expensively made of pine and then painted and which are coupled with plain or twisted balusters that support a sturdy handrail—these very different structural features for stairs add a special dimension to a country-style dwelling.

fireplaces
and stoves

Evolving from a crude hole in the wall, the simple rectilinear fire surround with a practical mantel shelf storing a host of useful items was constructed from a broad variety of materials—stone, wood, and marble as well as painted plaster and pine—and eventually moved from the kitchen to other parts of the house.

The age-old tradition of having a fireplace in bedrooms, sitting rooms, and libraries as well as the usual one in the kitchen has been embraced enthusiastically in modern times—especially by those looking to create an authentic country ambience. In addition to the fireplace, the clean and economical stove—especially favored in the country dwellings of northern Europe—holds pride of place as an important decorative feature when surrounded by tiles as well as providing the vital necessities of cooking, providing hot water, and bringing heat into the room.

In the French provinces of Brittany and Normandy, the stove is most likely to be set into an existing fireplace, while Sweden embraces the Scandinavian taste for tall cylindrical stoves completely clad with curved tiles. In America, the New England Shaker custom of positioning a plain cast-iron stove on legs in the center of the room continues to appeal for country-style homes today. And where a romantic open fireplace is not practical due to a lack of space or the demands of modern heating, the 21st-century kitchen can adopt a number of alternatives—from the English country kitchen with a gleaming and hot-round-the-clock Aga that has been placed in an alcove and surrounded by colorful tiles, to the minimalist simplicity of the Scandinavian waist-high hooded hearth, with slats that can accommodate a grill for cooking food.

furniture

In the furnishing and decoration of interiors that look to the pastoral aesthetic for inspiration, it is the ubiquitous chair that best sums up a country spirit founded upon the ideal of comfort and relaxation.

chairs

Traditionally a house located in the country played home to a hodge-podge of tables, chairs, and beds, which were constructed by local craftsmen from age-old designs that over the decades remained impervious to change. These furnishings—timeworn vernacular pieces that may have been lovingly handed down from one generation to the next—might be happily arranged alongside pieces collected over time from different periods as well as from a broad range of cultures. The solid, practical, and utilitarian furniture of the country has always played a pivotal role in the need to escape from the pressures of life from day to day by providing a sense of comfort, security, and solace. Today—in what seems to be an insensitive and occasionally dangerous world—it is the simplicity and humble character of country furniture that proffers a nurturing alternative to flashy and ephemeral extravagance.

Alongside the bed, the chair tends to hold pride of place—with good reason—as the most important item of furniture to be found in the home. From the Middle Ages the chair has been a symbol of both power and authority. Now in the 21st century the chair continues to touch the imagination, as it looks back to the past and the country philosophy to enhance the furnishing and decoration of an interior created to be a restful and comfortable sanctuary. Whether centered within a warm and

LEFT This 19th-century Norwegian country pine chair shows the many succesive layers of paint and varnish that have been applied over the years.

OPPOSITE, TOP FROM LEFT A late 18th-century English country oak chair, with pierced splat, sits in front of a dado rail with pine paneling. A simple late 19th- or early 20th-century French painted side chair, with characteristic heart-carved top rail. A 17th-century Spanish walnut country chair, with bobbin turning. OPPOSITE, CENTER FROM LEFT This mid-18th century English ash"stick" chair has lobster pot cresting on the back frame. The rich tones of this walnut early English open armchair, circa 1720–40, are complemented by the beautifully detailed *gros point* embroidered seat. Dug out from a massive piece of elm, it was made in the West Country of England in the first half of the 18th century. OPPOSITE, BOTTOM FROM LEFT A faux-painted side chair from the Hudson River Valley School, circa1880–90, with fake wood detailing. These "klismos"-style chairs were popular in New England circa 1820–40. A 19th- century English yew-wood low-back Windsor chair, with a spindle back and shaped seat circa 1830. An early 19th-century Swedish side chair, with original paint. This is a transitional piece, with the back displaying Gothic influence.

generous kitchen in the heart of a villa nestled in the Italian countryside that regularly celebrates life by playing host to a panoply of family and friends, or artfully arranged in the welcoming living room of a London townhouse stylishly decorated in a style that honors the best of forward-looking designs which are at once sleek, chic, and modern—the humble chair plays a dual role as a practical and decorative component of a pleasant and hospitable refuge from the outside world as well as a basic vehicle for leisure and relaxation.

History tells us that the design and construction of plain, utilitarian country chairs did not eschew decoration, with the flaws and imperfections inherent in the wood artfully disguised by painting patterns and designs that joyfully celebrate what has gone before. Throughout the centuries it is the chair that has tended to be a timeless and provocative reminder of power, an unpretentious symbol that simultaneously speaks to both the elegant world of kings and queens and to an audience of relatively modest means and more humble aspirations.

Throughout the centuries the chair also symbolizes the desire for comfort that lies at the heart of the country style. Foreign influences—such as the stylistic movements in France from the mid-17th to the end of the 18th century—coupled with its role as a functional piece of furniture that naturally lends itself to a host of imaginative designs and materials has seen the chair evolve dramatically. From the earliest oak benches and settles grew the fashion for elaborately carved walnut or mahogany armchairs and dining chairs often upholstered with rich velvets, silks, needlework textiles, or more humble materials such as leather, wicker, or rush. Over time chairs developed to boast ever more generous proportions to accommodate the growing appetite for comfort and ease. The clean lines, honesty of materials, and integrity of construction championed in the 19th century by the Arts and Crafts movement—as in the rush-bottomed Sussex chair created by William Morris—resonates in the 21st century with chairs that echo the simplicity and comfort demanded by modern interpretations of country style.

A house has been designed for living in, and a country dwelling is essentially created as a restful hideaway from the outside world. The fundamental appeal of the country philosophy that champions the home as a cozy and welcoming retreat lies in its interpretation of the desire for warmth and comfort. All rooms need some form of seating, and it is the chair that over the centuries has responded to this challenge by marrying the comfortable with the practical, the functional with the decorative. Where chairs meant for a kitchen, a dining room, or occasional spaces such as hallways and bedrooms tend to be made with or without arms in simple and durable shapes and with straight backs and the odd decorative cushion—those found in the living room will boast generous overstuffed armchairs with soft pillows to enhance the cocoonlike cozy atmosphere that has been created with an eye to pastimes such as reading, entertaining, and generally relaxing.

Just as different rooms require different kinds of chairs, the surrounding landscape also plays a key role in how chairs are used to furnish and decorate an interior that has been inspired by the country. In the spacious villas found in Italy, New Mexico, or Morocco, for example, the demand for a cool retreat from the sizzling temperatures will inevitably find chairs and sofas painted and upholstered in light, refreshing colors—white, cream, pale yellow—while in the cold Northern climates of Norway or upstate New York, chairs can bring additional warmth into a room when covered in rich, sumptuous shades—ruby red and persimmon, forest green and deep sapphire blue—and constructed of wood such as oak, pine, or elm that complement the wall paneling or wood plank floors.

The chair—as defined by the country aesthetic—tends to be constructed in plain, clean-lined shapes and made from natural materials—wood such as oak found in plentiful supply in the surrounding forests nearby or trees that dot the local landscape. In a traditional rustic country interior, pieces that reflect the timeless elegance found in a well-crafted Shaker rocking chair will mix happily side by side with the scarred patina of rough-hewn Swedish farm bench or an English combback Windsor chair made of ash or elm and covered with a timeworn handpainted finish. By contrast, a home that has been decorated with a modern approach to the ideals of country might be furnished with chairs boasting pure, clean minimalist lines that have been constructed from modern materials such as tubular steel or laminated plywood and embellished with seats covered in luxurious fabrics such as leather or velvet. Well-worn, comfortable chairs made of metal, wicker, or sun-bleached wood add a colorful dimension to a garden terrace or veranda, providing a pleasurable extension of the living room for relaxation and informal dining while celebrating a love for the outdoors that remains the very definition of a love for the spirit of the countryside.

RIGHT Antique French doors with original paint are reused to make a pantry in the old kitchen of this 19th-century Normandy coaching inn.

FAR RIGHT In the hall stands an Italian cabinet from the 17th century in walnut. It has a wonderful, warm patina. A substantial piece of furniture, it is an antique showpiece that provides ample storage.

storage

OPPOSITE A row of built-in cupboards, classically inspired in design and partly glazed, are painted to blend with the kitchen scheme, and contain a collection of creamware and drinking glasses.

It is in the traditional handcrafted furniture of the rural countryside, in designs that have evolved and adapted over centuries of practical use, where a host of imaginative and resourceful solutions can be found to the ever-present need for more storage space.

A modern urban apartment located high above a bustling New York City, an historic townhouse in the center of Stockholm, a cozy but small thatch-roofed cottage nestled in the English countryside, a spacious stone farmhouse in Provence, a whitewashed sun-drenched villa resting on a Spanish hillside—all of these very different dwellings dotted across the world share in common the contemporary need for more space for storage and a consensus that there never seems to be enough

of it. Even living in a house of size and spaciousness does not automatically imply that there will be more room for stashing what are considered to be the modest needs of the commonplace and the everyday; in reality the picture might be quite different.

Life in the 21st century in many ways mirrors life in the 15th century. That is, there has existed for centuries the need to find places and spaces to store, hide, and protect one's property. On the one hand, these possessions take the form of the indispensable human necessities that keep life running smoothly—so there developed hutches and pantries for the storage of food, pots and pans, and tableware, racks for bottles of wine, cupboards meant for clothing to wear, chests and coffers to hold blankets for keeping warm on a cold winter's night, caskets for hiding treasured valuables, chests that furnish ample room for towels, soaps, lotions, and potions, shelves for books and glass-fronted display cabinets to house precious collectibles. As the years have passed, so the kinds of storage required have naturally evolved and changed. Cupboards for clothing became built-in, walk-in closets, the humble coffer was turned into a sophisticated chest placed on a stand—a highboy or a chest-on-chest—boxes for silverware became drawers set into sideboards, a bureau plat or writing table metamorphosed into a complex rolltop desk, a filing cabinet or a work table for keeping ink and writing papers, embroidery or playing cards. Refrigerators for keeping food chilled, cellars for wine, trash containers for what was no longer needed—such novelties have been continuously created to address the burgeoning demands for storage spaces to meet specific requirements. In today's complex world even the most humble home needs adequate and dedicated storage space for such essentials as televisions, music systems, and computers.

The country house style offers a wide variety of canny options for storage, frequently taking inspiration from different countries around the globe and moving from one century to the next. Storage furniture such as the armoire rendered in the architectural forms that were highly fashionable in the 17th century, for example, still resonates today in sophisticated modern interpretations or in faithful copies that mingle happily together with favorite antiques. The decoration of a warm and cozy country-style interior looks back to and celebrates the values of the rural past that were borne from necessity, and the need for ample space to store one's belongings has remained constant throughout the ages. Holding pride of place in the country-inspired rooms of the 21st century ranging from Colorado to Norway, New Mexico to sunny Morocco are commodious armoires, cabinets, chests-of-drawers, hutches and chests that have been plainly constructed from local lumber in traditional vernacular shapes and decorated—with a raw, timeworn patina, occasionally painted in soft and delicate shades including gray, celery, cream, and blue, joyfully lavished with colorful folk patterns inspired by the surrounding landscape or in more sophisticated versions fashioned from expensive wood veneers such as walnut and mahogany. Although decorated with an eye to the country aesthetic that is founded upon comfort and relaxation, the modern interior cannot help but acknowledge the real need for storage space.

Throughout history, a shortage of space for living has necessarily posed a challenge when considering storage requirements. Today, accommodating the pressing need for a dedicated place for the deposit of everything from clothing and culinary equipment to books and computers is no less demanding and requires a healthy dose of creativity as well as imagination. Furnishings originally intended to play a storage role are often called upon to be useful in other ways and be decorative as well—a richly carved blanket chest doubles as a coffee or side table, a canterbury initially meant for holding sheets of music is transformed into a rack for storing magazines, an agricultural "ark," which was traditionally used for storing grain, becomes a convenient bench, a cube-shaped footstool converts into a commodious storage box.

Sharing the spotlight with case furniture such as cupboards, armoire and cabinets, built-in furniture that utilizes the architecture of a room—beds boasting storage chests beneath,

ABOVE Dominique Kieffer's utility room in Normandy has a simple gray linen and white color scheme. The draped linen conceals the appliances, and the chest was found by Dominique in the southwest of France; it was originally a seed chest.

OPPOSITE Coffers, blanket and dower chests were the earliest forms of storage. They were often painted and much prized by their owners, often young girls preparing for marriage. This example is Bohemian circa 1830 and has typical floral decoration.

corner cupboards for the display of china and glassware, closets wedged in the space beneath a staircase for hanging coats or holding brooms, mops and vaccuum cleaners, cabinets tucked into paneled alcoves for sheltering a music system or television and floor-to-ceiling bookcases built into niches surrounding a fireplace, for example—offer practical as well as decorative alternatives. Other methods of maximizing limited space for storage include using flat boxes that slide out of sight under a bed, curtains placed beneath sinks to disguise cupboard shelves hidden behind, hinged screens blocking the clutter and generous

LEFT This home in upstate New York was converted from mill workers cottages built in 1898. This painted side cupboard was the only piece of furniture remaining from that time.

BELOW, CLOCKWISE FROM LEFT In southern Spain and North Africa these simple baked-mud units provide ample storage. Here they are painted vivid Moroccan blue. In Normandy late 18th- century doors were restored to provide storage for antique glass and 19th-century creamware.

In a country kitchen it is not necessary to conceal everything: open shelves are stacked with antique English and French creamware. Hutches, whether old or new, can be the ideal kitchen storage solution. The dresser base is a very useful storage space (for concealing the wedding presents you hate, perhaps!) and the glazed upper section can display your china and glassware. In this Moroccan kitchen the flat gray painted field-paneled cupboards completely cover an end wall, providing ample storage. The run is broken by minaret-shaped open shelves. To maintain the almost monastic simplicity in this Pennsylvania stone cottage, a run of white lacquered units conceal deep pullout full-height shelves.

OPPOSITE In a modern country kitchen everything can be on display. Old bottles and wooden chopping boards become decorative features. Wicker baskets can hold everything from cookbooks to tablecloths.

cloths thrown over tables that successfully hide unsightly pots and pans, cleaning products, cans and jars of food, games and toys, books and files, and out-of-season clothing.

Still other, more humble yet no less effective means for solving the storage problem include woven baskets in varying sizes that are piled high with everything from towels and linens, fresh fruits and vegetables, newspapers and magazines, cooking utensils, dog toys or CDs, jars large and small for storing herbs, spices, and jams or rice and pasta, and colorful boxes to hold cosmetics and toiletries. Hanging cupboards and plate racks, hooks suspended from the kitchen ceiling to hold cookware and pegs for draping jackets and coats add a country sensibility while bringing additional innovative solutions for storage into both a small-spaced apartment in the center of a bustling city or into an expansive cabin nestled in the mountains.

artifacts

The memories of the past, and of special lives well-lived as reflected in commemorative decorative artifacts, are the particular ingredients that lend every country dwelling an atmosphere of highly original personal style.

By its very nature the decoration of a house that looks to the country ideal for inspiration calls forth a mood founded on the desire for comfort and relaxation, one that is miles away from the cares of today's hectic and unpredictable world. At once confident, yet simple and unpretentious, contemporary country style pays homage to age-old customs while remaining grounded in the 21st century. The modern interpretation of the country aesthetic celebrates the pleasures that are found in plain decoration while embracing the unique, the imperfect, and the unusual. Country style reveres the rural past and time-honored craftsmanship; it delights in objects boasting the beauty, purity and modesty born from homespun traditions.

In a country-inspired interior, decorative and ornamental objects tend to be of a practical and functional nature. Hand-

OPPOSITE Against the background of a rustic chinked wooden wall, old photographs are displayed in twig frames. The first is *Santa Clara Woman*, taken by H.T. Cory in 1916. The stick ladder frame contains from the top; *Winter, Apsaroke, Crow* by Edward S. Curtis 1908, *An Oasis in the Badlands, Red Hawk, Oglala Lakota* by Edward S. Curtis 1905 and *Piegan, Blackfoot*, by Roland Reed 1915.

RIGHT, CLOCKWISE FROM TOP LEFT An old treen (turned wooden) bowl on an Elizabethan oak refectory table. A Norwegian treen banded lidded tankard against local fieldstone with lichen. Two new turned wooden cups on pegs on Montana pine log walls. A Norwegian naïve painted cream pail and cover with moss-colored painted logs. A 19th-century nutmeg and bay leaf box, with a nutmeg grater on a modern butcher's block. An 18th-century treen bowl sits on a honed granite surface against Pennsylvania fieldstone.

hammered copper cookware, battered pewter candlesticks, woven baskets, cast-iron pots, a faded crewelwork quilt, gelatin and butter molds, and ceramic tableware in a variety of colorful patterns—these types of useful artifacts were originally created to satisfy the basic needs of life, and they proudly display the battle scars resulting from years of repeated use. While over time many such objects have surrendered their original functional purpose in favor of playing a decorative role in the furnishing of a room, others continue to be both useful and decorative. Plates for eating and cups for drinking, coverlets for keeping warm, stoneware storage jars to keep herbs and spices,

brass chandeliers and copper lanterns for providing light, copper pots used for cooking, and rough-hewn wooden bowls hold fresh fruits and vegetables—when imaginatively arranged as decoration on a kitchen shelf or lining a cupboard, on a table, hung from a ceiling beam, across a wall, or over a bed they add warmth and charm to any room.

Satisfaction comes from bringing together a variety of objects from different countries and periods, by honoring their inherent beauty and paying tribute to the fine craftsmanship of centuries past. The display of inherited family treasures, precious collections lovingly assembled over the years or highly prized

CLOCKWISE FROM TOP LEFT An irregular eathernware vessel, displayed against the distressed walls of this timber-paneled room, offers a seamless homage to the past. A Hopi ceramic bowl from northeastern Arizona is decorated with geometric patterns. The Hopi design vocabulary is usually abstract bird images, wings, and feathers rendered in geometric fashion. Birds are sacred to the Hopi who believe they carry people's prayers to heaven. The texture of this regular stone wheel, whose former use may have been to grind local grain, is in keeping with the rough hue of the vertical stone slabs that comprise the simple fire surround below. A pre-Columbian Anasazi ceramic bowl from the southwest.

OPPOSITE The interior of the Anasazi bowl showing "the Thunderbird"—a potent symbol for the tribe.

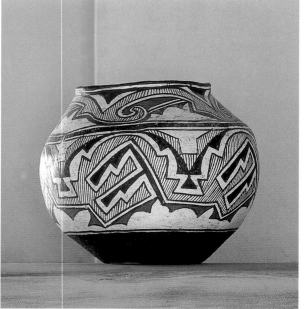

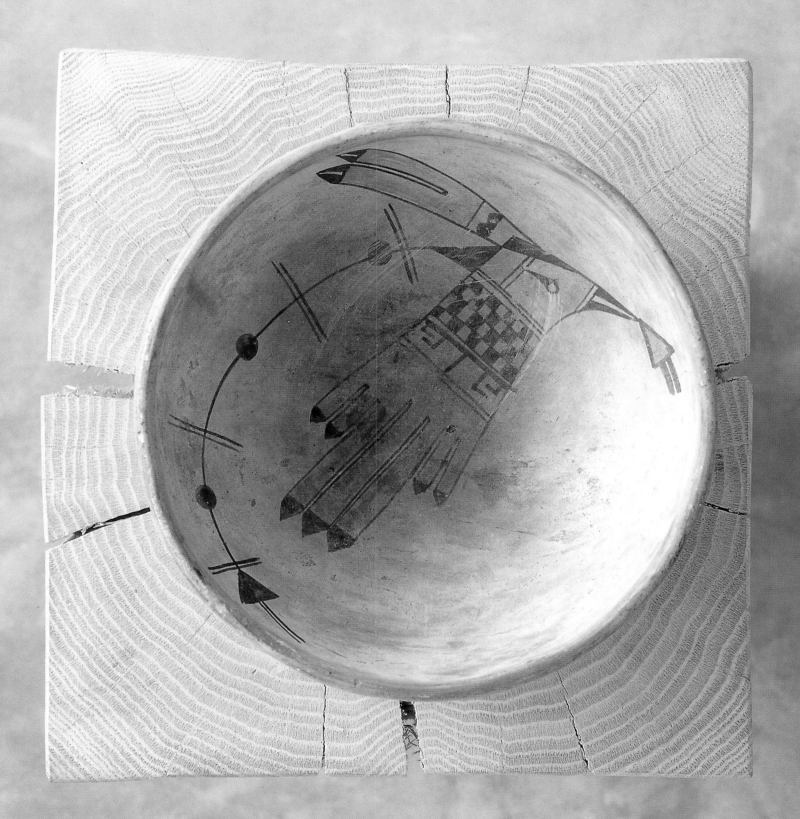

OPPOSITE, CLOCKWISE FROM TOP LEFT
Tin-glazed earthenware dishes make
the perfect containers for nuts and
herbs. Against a wooden plank wall
a collection of tin-glazed earthenware
pots sit on an old pine scalloped
shelf. Among the strainers is a
collection of *trouvés*—a large leaf of
Gunnera mannicata and a wonderfully
gnarled wooden root. Running a
working farm in upstate New York
means that Chris Bortugno is never
short of eggs taken daily from the
hens and freshly dug potatoes and
picked cabbage cooked in old copper
pans on an ancient range. The stuff of
country reverie! A useful collection of
tools and cooking herbs gathered in
one place—utility and aesthetics
combined are the country ideal.

ABOVE There is a reassuring
connection with the past in this
cameo collection of early 19th-
century American stoneware ovoid
jugs in the summer kitchen of a 1735
Connecticut house. Most of them
were made by firms in Connecticut.

bibelots that hold cherished memories of vacation travels are
other kinds of decorative artefacts that reflect the country
aesthetic of a warm and friendly environment by bringing a
sense of the unique and personal into the decoration of a room.

The search for unpretentious simplicity and the absence of
decorative trappings and Victorian clutter that are the hallmarks
of the Arts and Crafts movement are equally at home with the
ease and comfort of country-style living in the 21st century. The
spartan comfort of the Arts and Crafts interior—defined by a
minimum of ornamental artefacts that are nearly always
functional and crafted by hand—is frequently shared by the its
modern counterpart, which prefers to remain devoid of
extraneous embellishments and concentrate on purity of form.

Functional objects that have been used to decorate an
interior have an innocent charm and appeal that speaks to the
desire for a relaxing and comforting refuge. Country-inspired
style finds and celebrates what is special, unique, and beautiful
in ordinary everyday objects that have defied the passage of time,
and it remains equally at home in a cabin hideaway, a sun-baked
retreat, or a sleek modern high-rise apartment.

suppliers

furniture and other furnishings

specialist retailers & dealers

Andrew Martin International Ltd
(See Fabrics and Wallpapers for contact details)

Beaumont & Fletcher
261 Fulham Road
London SW3 6HY, UK
Tel: +44 (0)20 7352 5594
www.beaumontandfletcher.com
Distributed in the USA via F. Schumacher & Co
(See Fabrics and Wallpapers for contact details)

The Blue Pump
178 Davenport Road
Toronto M5R 1J2, Canada
Tel: +1 416 944 1673
www.thebluepump.com

Brunschwig & Fils Inc.
(See Fabrics and Wallpapers for contact details)

David Champion
199 Westbourne Grove
London W11 2SB, UK
Tel: +44 (0)20 7727 6016

The Country Seat
Huntercombe Manor Barn
Nr Henley on Thames, RG9 5RY, UK
Tel: +44 (0)1491 641349
www.thecountryseat.com

Donghia Furniture/Textiles Ltd.
485 Broadway, New York, NY 10013
Tel: +1 (212) 925 2777
www.donghia.com
Also at:
Donghia UK Ltd
23 Chelsea Harbour Design Centre
London SW10 0XE, UK
Tel: +44 (0)20 7823 3456

Fay Gold Gallery
764 Miami Circle
Atlanta, GA 30324
Tel: +1 404 233 3843
www.faygoldgallery.com

Josephine Ryan Antiques & Interiors
63 Abbeville Road, London SW4 9JW, UK
Tel: +44 (0)20 8675 3900
www.josephineryanantiques.co.uk

Lowe Gallery
Space A02
75 Bennett Street
Atlanta, GA 30324
Tel: +1 (404) 352 8114
www.lowegallery.com

Mark Maynard Antiques
651 Fulham Road
London SW6 5PU
Tel: +44 (0)20 7731 3533
www.markmaynard.co.uk

Nobilis
(see Fabrics and Wallpapers for contact details)

Tobias and the Angel
68 Whitehart Lane
Barnes, London SW13 0PZ, UK
Tel: +44 (0)208 878 8902
www.tobiasandtheangel.com

auction houses

David Rago Auctions
333 North Main Street
Lambertville, NJ 08530
Tel: +1 (609) 397 9374
www.ragoarts.com

Dreweatt Neate
Donnington Priory Salerooms
Donnington
Newbury
Berkshire RG14 2JE, UK
Tel: +44 (0)1635 553553
www.dreweatt-neate.co.uk

Freemans
1808 Chestnut Street,
PA 19103
Tel: +1 (215) 563 9275
www.freemansauction.com

Lots Road Auctions
71–73 Lots Road, Chelsea,
London SW10 0RN, UK
Tel: +44 (0)20 7351 7771
www.lotsroad.com

Lyon and Turnbull
33 Broughton Place,
Edinburgh EH1 3RR, UK
Tel: +44 (0)131 557 8844
www.lyonandturnbull.com

Pook & Pook
463 East Lancaster Avenue
Downington, PA 19335
Tel: +1 (610) 269 4040
www.pookandpook.com

Skinner Auctions Inc.
63 Park Plaza
Boston, MA 02116
Tel: +1 (617) 350 5429
www.skinnerinc.com

Woolley & Wallis
51-61 Castle Street, Salisbury
Wiltshire SP1 3SU, UK
Tel: +44 (0)1722 424500
www.woolleyandwallis.co.uk

architectural salvage

Antique Architecture
E. P. F. O. Imports Inc.
6152 Wenrich Drive
San Diego, CA 92120
Tel: +1 (619) 583 3791
www.ancientarchitecture.com

Architectural Emporium
207 Adams Avenue
Canonsburg, PA 15317
Tel: +1 724 746 4301
www.architectural-emporium.com

The Architectural Reclaim Centre
New Barn, Cock Lane
Highwood, Essex, CM1 3RB, UK
Tel: +44 (0)1277 354777
www.architecturalreclaim.com

Architiques
35 Otsego Street
Oneonta, NY 13820
Tel: +1 (607) 432 9890
www.architiques.net

Lassco
St Michael's Church, Mark Street
London EC2 4ER, UK
Tel: +44 (0)207 7499944
www.lassco.co.uk

Walcot Reclamation
108 Walcot Street, Bath BA1 5BG, UK
Tel: +44 (0)1225 44404
www.walcotreclamation.com

fabrics and wallpapers

Alexander Beauchamp
Appleby Business Centre
Appleby Street, Blackburn
Lancashire BB1 3BL, UK
Tel: +1 (0)1254 691133
www.alexanderbeauchamp.com
*(Available in the USA via the
D & D Building)*

Andrew Martin International Ltd
200 Walton Street
London SW3 2JL, UK
Tel: +44 (0)20 7225 5100
www.andrewmartin.co.uk
Also at:
D&D Annex, 222 East 59th Street
New York, NY 10022
Tel: +1 (212) 688 4297

Baer & Ingram
Dragon Works, Leigh on Mendip
Radstock BA53 5QZ, UK
Tel: +44 (0)1373 813800
Also at:
Davan Port Ltd
404 Pleasant View Court
Copague, NY 11726
Tel: +1 (631) 225 1811
www.baer-ingram.com

Beaumont & Fletcher
(See Furniture for contact details)

Brunschwig & Fils Inc.
10, The Chambers
Chelsea Harbour Drive,
London SW10 OXF, UK
Tel: +44 (0)20 7351 5797
Also at:
75 Virginia Road
North White Plains, NY 10603
+1 (914) 872-1100
www.brunschwig.com

Celia Birtwell
71 Westbourne Park Road
London W2 5QH, UK
Tel: +44 (0)20 7221 0877
www.celiabirtwell.com

Claremont Furnishing Fabrics Co. Ltd
35 Elystan Street
London SW3 3NT, UK
Tel: +44 (0)20 7581 9675
www.claremontfurnishing.com
Also at:
2nd Floor, 1059 Third Avenue,
New York, NY 10021
Tel: +1 (212) 486 1252

Colefax and Fowler
19-23 Grosvenor Hill
London W1X 3QD, UK
Tel: +44 (0)20 7318 6000
www.colefax.com

Crowson
227 Kings Road
London SW3 5EJ, UK
Tel: +44 (0)20 7376 7767
www.crowsonfabrics.com

D & D Building
979 Third Avenue
New York, NY10022
Tel: +1 (212) 759 2964
www.ddbuilding.com

Donghia Furniture/Textiles Ltd
(For contact details See Furniture section)

F. Schumacher & Co.
Suite 832, D & D Building
(See above for full address)
Tel: +1 (212) 415 3900
www.fschumacher.com
(Visit website for international retailers)

G. P. & J. Baker
2 Stinsford Road, Poole
Dorset BH17 OSW, UK
Tel: +44 (0)1202 266700
www.gpjbaker.co.uk
Distributed in the USA via Lee Joffa
(See below for contact details)

Ian Mankin
109 Regents Park Road
Primrose Hill, London NW1 8UR, UK
Tel: +44 (0)20 7722 0997
www.ianmankin.com

JAB International Furnishing Ltd
1/15–16 Chelsea Harbour Design Centre
London SW10 OXE, UK
Tel: +44 (0)20 7349 9323
Also at:
155 East 56th Street
New York, NY10022
Tel: +1 (212) 486 1500
www.jab.de

Lee Jofa
Unit 5, Knighton Heath Industrial Estate
851 Ringwood Road, Bournemouth
Dorset BH11 8NE, UK
Tel: +44 (0)1202 575 457
Also at:
201 Central Avenue South,
Bethpage, New York, NY 11714
Tel: +1 (516) 752 7600

Malabar
31-33, The South Bank Business Centre
Ponton Road, London SW8 5BL, UK
Tel: +44 (0)20 7501 4200
www.malabar.co.uk
Also at:
8a Trowbridge Drive
Bethel, CT 06801
Tel: +1 (877) 625 2227

Nobilis
Bellevue House, Althorp Road
London SW17 7ED, UK
Tel: +44 (0)20 8767 0774
www.nobilis.fr
Also at:
20 Locust Avenue
Berkley Heights,
New Jersey, NY 07922
Tel: +1 (908) 464 1177

Osborne & Little
304 King's Road
London SW3 5UH, UK
Tel: +44 (0)20 7352 1456
www.osborneandlittle.com
Also at:
979 Third Avenue, Suite 520,
New York, NY 10022
Tel: +1 (212) 751 333

Sahco Hesslein
G24 Chelsea Harbour Design Centre
London SW10 OXE, UK
Tel: +44 (0)20 7352 6168
Also at:
Bergamo Fabrics Inc.,
D&D Building, 17th Floor
979 Third Avenue
New York, NY 10022
Tel: +1 (212) 888 333
www.sacho-hesslein.com

Sanderson
100 Acres, Sanderson Road
Uxbridge, Middlesex
UB8 1DH, UK
Tel: +44 (0)1895 830044
www.sanderson-online.co.uk
Also at:
285 Grand Avenue,
3 Patriot Centre,
Englewood, New Jersey, NY 07631
Tel: +1 800 894 6185

Scalamandré
300 Trade Zone Drive
Ronkonkoma
New York, NY 11779
Tel: +1 (631) 467 8800
www.scalamandre.com

Also at:
Unit G-4, Chelsea Harbour Design Centre
Lots Road, London SW10 OXE, UK
Tel: +44 (0)20 7795 0988

Warner Fabrics
Unit G11, Chelsea Harbour Design Centre
London SW10 OXE, UK
Tel: +44 (0)20 8971 1716
www.warnerfabrics.com
Distributed in the USA via Lee Joffa

Zimmer & Rohde
15 Chelsea Harbour Design Centre
London SW10 OXE, UK
Tel: +44 (0)20 7351 7115
Also at:
15 Commerce Road
Stamford, CT 06902
Tel: +1 (203) 327 1400
www.zimmer-rohde.com

Zoffany
G9 Chelsea Harbour Design Centre
London SW10 OXE, UK
Tel: +44 (0)20 7349 0043
Also at:
Suite 1403, D & D Building
979 Third Avenue
New York, NY 10022
Tel: +1 (212) 593 9787
www.zoffany.com

Zuber
200 East 59th Street
New York, NY 75003
Tel: +1 (212) 486 9296
Also at:
42 Pimlico Road
London SW1 8LP, UK
Tel: +44 (0)20 7824 82 65

tiles and flooring

Amtico
Kingfield Road,
Coventry CV6 5AA, UK
Tel: +44 (0)2476 861400
www.amtico.com
Also at:
The Amtico Studio
200 Lexington Avenue (32nd Street)
New York, NY 10016
Tel: +1 (212) 545 1127

Ann Sacks
5 East 16th Street
New York, NY 10003
Tel: +1 (800) 278 8453
www.annsacks.com

Bruce Hardwood Floors
185 Milton Park, Abingdon
Oxfordshire, OX14 4SR, UK
Tel: +44 (0)1235 515100
www.brucefloors.com
Also at:
16803 Dallas Parkway
Addison, TX 75001

Crucial Trading
PO Box 10469
Birmingham B46 1WB, UK
Tel: +44 (0)1675 743747
www.crucial-trading.com
Also at:
Concepts International
83 Harbour Road
Port Washington, NY 11050
Tel: +1 (516) 767 1110
Also distributed via:
Stark Carpet Corporation
(See below for contact details)

Dal-Tile Corporation
7834 C.F. Hawn Freeway
Dallas, TX 75217
Tel: +1 (214) 398 1411
www.daltile.com

Fired Earth
*(See Paints, Stains and Waxes section
for contact details)*

H&R Johnson Tiles Ltd
Harewood Street, Tunstall
Stoke on Trent
Staffordshire ST6 6JZ, UK
Tel: +44 (0)1782 575575
www.johnson-tiles.com
Also at:
H&R Johnson USA
122 Tice Lanes,
East Brunswick
New Jersey, NY 08816
Tel: +1 (732) 698 0900

Historic Floors of Oshkosh
911 East Main Street,
Winneconne, WI 45986
Tel: +1 (920) 582 9977
www.oshkosh.com

Junckers Hardwood
Wheaton Court, Commercial Centre
Wheaton Road, Witham
Essex CM8 3UJ, UK
Tel: +44 (0)1376 534700
www.junckershardwood.co.uk
Also at:
4920 East Landon Drive
Anaheim, CA 92807
Tel: +1 (800) 878 9663
www.junkershardwood.com

Kentucky Wood Floors
15412 Highway 62,
Charleston, IN 47111
Tel: +1 (502) 451 6024
www.kentuckywood.com
Also at:
Rainleaf Flooring
1 Bridge Street, Bures
Suffolk CO8 5AD, UK
Tel: +44 (0)1787 229986
www.rainleaf.com

Kirkstone
128 Walham Green Court
Moore Park Road, Fulham
London SW6 4DG
Tel: +44 (0)207 381 0424
www.kirkstone.com
Distributed in the USA via
Walker Zanger *(See below)*

Paris Ceramics
583 Kings Road
London SW6 2EH, UK
Tel: +44 (0)207 371 7778
www.parisceramics.com
Also at:
150 East 58th Street, 7th Floor,
New York, NY 10155
Tel: +1 (212) 644 2782

Stark Carpet
D & D Building, 11th Floor
979 Third Avenue
New York, NY 10022-1276
Tel: +1 (212) 752 9000
www.starkcarpet.com
Also at:
3/6–7 Chelsea Harbour Design Centre
3rd Floor, South Dome
Lots Road, London
SW10 OXE, UK
Tel: +44 (0)20 7352 6001

The Alternative Flooring Company
Unit 3b, Stephenson Close,
East Portway Industrial Estate,
Andover, Hampshire, SP10 3RU, UK
Tel: +44 (0)1264 335111
www.alternative-flooring.co.uk

Ulster Carpets
Castleisland Factory,
Craigavon BT62 1EE
Northern Ireland, UK
Tel: +44 (0)2838 334433
Also at:
Ulsters Carpet Mills (NA) Inc.
81 Whitlock Avenue
Marietta, GA 30064
Tel: +1 (770) 514 0707
www.ulstercarpets.com

Wicanders
Amorim (UK) Ltd
Suite 1EA, Bishops Weald House
Albion Way, Horsham
West Sussex RH12 1AH, UK
Tel: +44 (0)1403 710001
www.wicanders.com
Also at:
Amorim Cork America Inc.
2557 Napa Valley, Corporate Drive
Napa, CA 94558
Tel: +1 (707) 224 6000

paints, stains and waxes

Auro Organic Paints
Cheltenham Road, Bisley
Nr Stroud, Gloucestershire
GL6 7BX, UK
Tel: +44 (0)1452 772020
www.auro.co.uk
Also at:
1340-G Industrial Avenue,
Petaluma, CA 94952
Tel: +1 (707) 763 0662

Bleus de Pastel de Lectoure
Ancienne Tannerie, Pont de Pile
32700 Lectoure, France
Tel: +33 5 62 68 78 30
www.bleu-de-lectoure.com

Craig & Rose
Unit 8, Halbeath Industrial Estate
Dunfermline, Fife KY11 7EG,
Scotland, UK
Tel: +44 (0)870 600 1829
www.craigandrose.com

Crown
PO Box 37, Crown House
Hollins Road, Darwen
Lancashire, BB3 0BG, UK
Tel: +44 (0)1254 704951
www.crownpaint.co.uk
Also at:
Akzo Decorative Coatings Inc.
117 Brush Street
Poniac, MI 48341
Tel: +1 (248) 253 2496
www.akzonobel.com

Dulux
Dulux Customer Care Centre
ICI Paints, Wexham Road
Slough SL2 5DS, UK
Tel: +44 (0)1753 550000/555
www.dulux.com
Also at:
ICI Paints
925 Euclid Avenue
Cleveland, OH 44115
Tel: +1 (216) 344 8000
www.icidulux.com

Farrow & Ball
Uddens Trading Estate, Wimborne
Dorset BH21 7NL, UK
Tel: +44 (0)1202 876141
www.farrow-ball.com
(In addition to offering a direct delivery service overseas, they also list on their website their stockists in USA, Canada, Australia, New Zealand, Japan, Russia, and throughout continental Europe)

Fired Earth
Twyford Mill, Oxford Road
Adderbury, Oxon OX17 3HP, UK
Tel: +44 (0)12595 814399
www.firedearth.com

Holkham Linseed Paints
The Clock Tower, Longlands,
Holkham, Wells-Next-The-Sea,
Norfolk NR23 1RU, UK
Tel: +44 (0)1328 711348
www.holkham.co.uk

John Oliver Ltd
33 Pembridge Road,
London W11 3HG, UK
Tel: +44 (0)20 7221 6466
www.johnoliver.co.uk

Liberon Waxes Ltd
Mountfield Industrial Estate
Learoyd Road, New Romney
Kent TN28 8XU, UK
Tel: +44 (0)1797 367555
www.liberonltd.co.uk
Also at:
Liberon/Star Wood Finish Supply
PO Box 86
Mendocino, CA 95460
Tel: +1 (707) 962 9480
www.liberonsupply.com

The Old Fashioned Milk Paint Company
436 Main Street, PO Box 222
Groton, MA 01450
Tel: +1 (978) 448 6336
www.milkpaint.com

Old Village Paints
PO Box 1030
Fort Washington, PA 19034
Tel: +1 (610) 238 9001
www.old-village.com

Paint & Paper Library
David Oliver Ltd, 5 Elystan Street
London SW3 3NT, UK
Tel: +44 (0)20 7823 7755
www.paintlibrary.co.uk
Distributed in the USA via:
Stark Wallcovering
D&D Building, 979 3rd Avenue,
New York, NY 10022
Tel: +1 212 752 9000 Ext. 132

Papers and Paints Ltd
4 Park Walk, Chelsea
London SW10 0AD, UK
Tel: +44 (0)20 7352 8626
www.papers-paints.co.uk

Rose of Jericho
Horchester Farm, Holywell
Nr Evershot, Dorchester
Dorset DT2 0LL, UK
Tel: +44 (0)1935 83676
www.rose-of-jericho.demon.co.uk

index

Figures in *italics* refer to captions.

acknowledgments

Endpapers: *Front* Axel Vervoordt's house in Belgium *Back* Agnès Emery's house in Marrakech

1 Axel Vervoordt's house in Belgium; 2-3 Wingate Jackson, Jr and Paul Trantanella's house in upstate New York; 4-5 Tigmi, Morocco, designed by Max Lawrence; 8 Chris Bortugno's house in upstate New York; 9 a house in Connecticut designed by Jeffrey Bilhuber; 10 above left Mr & Mrs Sagbakken's cabin by the sea (Norway), interior design by Helene Forbes-Hennie; 10 above right Mr & Mrs Stokke's cabin in the Norwegian mountains, interior design by Helene Forbes-Hennie; 10 center left Chris Bortugno's house in upstate New York; 10 center Wingate Jackson, Jr and Paul Trantanella's house in upstate New York; 10 center right Fritz & Dana Rohn's Connecticut house; 10 below left Julie Prisca's house in Normandy; 10 below center a house in Provence designed by Jean-Louis Raynaud & Kenyon Kramer; 10 below right Tigmi, Morocco, designed by Max Lawrence; 14-15 a mountain retreat in Colorado, designed by Ron Mason; 16 Mrs Fasting's cabin in the Norwegian mountains, interior design by Heiberg Cummings Design; 17 a cabin in Aspen, designed by Holly Lueders; 18 above a house in Virginia designed by Solis Betancourt; 18 below Mrs Fasting's cabin in the Norwegian mountains, interior design by Heiberg Cummings Design; 19 above left a mountain retreat in Colorado, designed by Ron Mason; 19 above right left Mr & Mrs Sagbakken's cabin by the sea (Norway), interior design by Helene Forbes-Hennie; 19 below right Fritz & Dana Rohn's Connecticut house; 20 above left Alex van de Walle's apartment in Brussels; 20 above right Mr & Mrs Sagbakken's cabin by the sea (Norway), interior design by Helene Forbes-Hennie; 20 below left a house in Oxfordshire designed by Todhunter Earle; 20 below right Wingate Jackson, Jr and Paul Trantanella's house in upstate New York; 21 above Architect Gilles Pellerin's house in Cannes; 21 below a mountain retreat in Colorado, designed by Ron Mason; 22 a mountain retreat in Colorado, designed by Ron Mason; 23 a house in New Mexico, designed by Alexandra Champalimaud; 24-29 a mountain retreat in Colorado, designed by Ron Mason; 30-33 a house in Virginia designed by Solis Betancourt; 34-37 a house in New Mexico, designed by Alexandra Champalimaud; 38-41 Mrs Fasting's cabin in the Norwegian mountains, interior design by Heiberg Cummings Design; 42 Mr & Mrs Stokke's cabin in the Norwegian mountains, interior design by Helene Forbes-Hennie; 43 a house in Virginia designed by Solis Betancourt; 44 above left a house in Connecticut designed by Jeffrey Bilhuber; 44 above right Ali Sharland's house in Gloucestershire; 44 below left Tigmi, Morocco, designed by Max Lawrence; 44 below right a farmhouse near Toulouse designed by Kathryn Ireland; 45 Architect Gilles Pellerin's house in Cannes; 46 above Anthony Hudson's barn in Norfolk (photograph by Andrew Wood); 46 below James Gager & Richard Ferretti's Pennsylvanian house; 47 Mr & Mrs Boucquiau's house in Belgium, designed by Marina Frisenna (photograph by Andrew Wood); 48 above Mrs Fasting's cabin in the Norwegian mountains, interior design by Heiberg Cummings Design; 48 below Fritz & Dana Rohn's Connecticut house; 49 a cabin in Aspen, designed by Holly Lueders; 50-53 James Gager & Richard Ferretti's Pennsylvanian house; 54-57 a house in Connecticut designed by Jeffrey Bilhuber; 58-61 a farmhouse near Toulouse designed by Kathryn Ireland; 62 Ivy Ross & Brian Gill's home in Galisteo; 63 Tigmi, Morocco, designed by Max Lawrence; 64 above Ivy Ross & Brian Gill's home in Galisteo; 64 below Agnès Emery's house in Marrakech; 65 above left Ivy Ross & Brian Gill's home in Galisteo; 65 above right Peter and Marijke de Wit of Domaine d'Heerstaayen in the Netherlands; 65 below left Axel Vervoordt's house in Belgium; 65 below right Tigmi, Morocco, designed by Max Lawrence; 66 above left Axel Vervoordt's house in Belgium; 66 above right Ivy Ross & Brian Gill's home in Galisteo; 66 below left Ivy Ross & Brian Gill's home in Galisteo; 66 below right Agnès Emery's house in Marrakech; 67 Agnès Emery's house in Marrakech; 68 Tigmi, Morocco, designed by Max Lawrence; 69 Ivy Ross & Brian Gill's home in Galisteo; 70-73 Tigmi, Morocco, designed by Max Lawrence; 74-77 Ivy Ross & Brian Gill's home in Galisteo; 78-81 Peter and Marijke de Wit of Domaine d'Heerstaayen in the Netherlands; 82-83 Architect Gilles Pellerin's house in Cannes; 84-85 a house in Provence designed by Jean-Louis Raynaud & Kenyon Kramer; 86 Le Pavillion Levant designed by Jean-Louis Raynaud & Kenyon Kramer; 87 a house in Provence designed by Jean-Louis Raynaud & Kenyon Kramer; 88 Julie Prisca's house in

Normandy; 89 above Eric & Gloria Stewart's manor house in south-western France; 89 below left a house in Provence designed by Jean-Louis Raynaud & Kenyon Kramer; 89 below right Le Pavillion Levant designed by Jean-Louis Raynaud & Kenyon Kramer; 90 below a house in Italy designed by Ilaria Miani; 91 a house in Italy designed by Ilaria Miani; 92-93 a house in Italy designed by Anthony Collett; 94 Martine Colliander of White Sense's apartment in Stockholm, Sweden; 95 above left & below Marianne von Kantzow of Solgården's house in Stockholm; 95 above right Mrs Fasting's cabin in the Norwegian mountains, interior design by Heiberg Cummings Design; 96 above Mrs Fasting's cabin in the Norwegian mountains, interior design by Heiberg Cummings Design; 96 below Marianne von Kantzow of Solgården's house in Stockholm; 97-98 Mr & Mrs Sagbakken's cabin by the sea (Norway), interior design by Helene Forbes-Hennie; 99 above Mr & Mrs Stokke's cabin in the Norwegian mountains, interior design by Helene Forbes-Hennie; 99 below Mrs Fasting's cabin in the Norwegian mountains, interior design by Heiberg Cummings Design; 100 above a house in Oxfordshire designed by Todhunter Earle; 100 below Robert & Josyane Young's home in London; 101 a house in Oxfordshire designed by Todhunter Earle; 102 Ali Sharland's house in Gloucestershire; 103 Robert & Josyane Young's house in London; 104 above Michael Leva's house in Connecticut; 104 below a house in Water Mill, Long Island, designed by Naomi Leff & Associates; 105 a cabin in Aspen, designed by Holly Lueders; 106-107 Fritz & Dana Rohn's Connecticut house; 108 above Pamela Kline (of Traditions)'s home in Claverack, New York; 108 below a house in Connecticut designed by Jeffrey Bilhuber; 109 Fritz & Dana Rohn's Connecticut house; 110 above Tigmi, Morocco, designed by Max Lawrence; 110 below Riyad Edward in Marrakech designed by Stephen Skinner; 111 Riyad Edward in Marrakech designed by Stephen Skinner; 112-113 Agnès Emery's house in Marrakech; 114-117 a house in Connecticut designed by Jeffrey Bilhuber; 118 above Axel Vervoodt's house in Belgium; 118 below a farmhouse near Toulouse designed by Kathryn Ireland; 119 Architect Gilles Pellerin's house in Cannes; 120 above left Julie Prisca's house in Normandy; 120 above right Mr & Mrs Stokke's cabin in the Norwegian mountains, interior design by Helene Forbes-Hennie; 120 below left Frank Faulkner's house in upstate New York; 120 below right a house in Oxfordshire designed by Todhunter Earle; 121 a mountain retreat in Colorado, designed by Ron Mason; 122 above Alex van de Walle's apartment in Brussels; 122 below Agnès Emery's house in Marrakech; 123 Agnès Emery's house in Marrakech; 124 above left Agnès Emery's house in Marrakech; 124 above right Mr & Mrs Sagbakken's cabin by the sea (Norway), interior design by Helene Forbes-Hennie; 124 below left Agnès Emery's house in Marrakech; 124 below right Peter and Marijke de Wit of Domaine d'Heerstaayen in the Netherlands; 125 Architect Gilles Pellerin's house in Cannes; 126 Julie Prisca's house in Normandy; 127 Mr & Mrs Stokke's cabin in the Norwegian mountains, interior design by Helene Forbes-Hennie; 128 left Dominique Kieffer's house in Normandy; 128-129 a house in Provence designed by Jean-Louis Raynaud & Kenyon Kramer; 130 above left Peter and Marijke de Wit of Domaine d'Heerstaayen in the Netherlands; 130 above right Agnès Emery's house in Marrakech; 130 below left Architect Gilles Pellerin's house in Cannes; 130 below right Frank Faulkner's house in upstate New York; 131 above Ivy Ross & Brian Gill's home in Galisteo; 131 below Agnès Emery's house in Marrakech; 132 above left Peter and Marijke de Wit of Domaine d'Heerstaayen in the Netherlands; 132 below left a house in Oxfordshire designed by Todhunter Earle; 132-133 Axel Vervoodt's house in Belgium; 134 Michael Leva's house in Connecticut; 135 Frank Faulkner's house in upstate New York; 136-137 Dominique Kieffer's house in Normandy; 137 above a house in New Mexico, designed by Alexandra Champalimaud; 137 below a farmhouse near Toulouse designed by Kathryn Ireland; 138 above Fritz & Dana Rohn's Connecticut house; 138 below Mr & Mrs Sagbakken's cabin by the sea (Norway), interior design by Helene Forbes-Hennie; 139 above left Architect Gilles Pellerin's house in Cannes; 139 above right Mr & Mrs Stokke's cabin in the Norwegian mountains, interior design by Helene Forbes-Hennie; 139 below left & right Agnès Emery's house in Marrakech; 140 above left a cabin in Aspen, designed by Holly Lueders; 140 above right a house in Connecticut designed by Jeffrey Bilhuber; 140 below a mountain retreat in Colorado, designed by Ron Mason; 141 Alex van de Walle's apartment in Brussels; 142 Architect Gilles Pellerin's house in Cannes; 143 Mr & Mrs Stokke's cabin in the Norwegian mountains, interior design by Helene Forbes-Hennie; 144 above left & center Agnès Emery's house in Marrakech; 144 above right Peter and Marijke de Wit of Domaine d'Heerstaayen in the Netherlands; 144 below Dominique Kieffer's house in Normandy; 145 above left Architect Gilles Pellerin's house in Cannes; 145 above center a mountain retreat in Colorado, designed by Ron Mason; 145 above right James Gager & Richard Ferretti's Pennsylvanian house; 145 below Ivy Ross & Brian Gill's home in Galisteo; 146-147 Axel Vervoodt's house in Belgium; 148 above Tigmi, Morocco, designed by Max Lawrence; 148 below Axel Vervoodt's house in Belgium; 149 left Ali Sharland's house in Gloucestershire; 150 above Dominique Kieffer's house in Normandy; 150 below Fritz & Dana Rohn's Connecticut house; 151 Agnès Emery's house in Marrakech; 152 A mountain retreat in Colorado, designed by Ron Mason; 153 above a cabin in Aspen, designed by Holly Lueders; 153 below Mr & Mrs Stokke's cabin in the Norwegian mountains, interior design by Helene Forbes-Hennie; 154-155 Agnès Emery's house in Marrakech; 156 above Axel Vervoodt's house in Belgium; 156 below Agnès Emery's house in Marrakech; 157 above a house in Provence designed by Jean-Louis Raynaud & Kenyon Kramer; 157 below Ali Sharland's house in Gloucestershire; 158 above Michael Leva's house in Connecticut; 158 below James Gager & Richard Ferretti's Pennsylvanian house; 159-160 Architect Gilles Pellerin's house in Cannes; 161 above left Ivy Ross & Brian Gill's home in Galisteo; 161 above center Axel Vervoodt's house in Belgium; 161 above right Tigmi, Morocco, designed by Max Lawrence; 161 center left Mr & Mrs Sagbakken's cabin by the sea, interior design by Helene Forbes-Hennie; 161 center Agnès Emery's house in Marrakech; 161 center right Axel Vervoodt's house in Belgium; 161 below left Axel Vervoodt's house in Belgium; 161 below center Architect Gilles Pellerin's house in Cannes; 161 below right Agnès Emery's house in Marrakech; 162 above left Dominique Kieffer's house in Normandy; 162 above center a farmhouse near Toulouse designed by Kathryn Ireland; 162 above right Chris Bortugno's house in upstate New York; 162 center left Mary Mullane's house in Claverack, New York; 162 center Agnès Emery's house in Marrakech; 162 center right Julie Prisca's house in Normandy; 162 below left James Gager & Richard Ferretti's Pennsylvanian house; 162 below center Alex van de Walle's apartment in Brussels; 162 below right a house in Connecticut designed by Jeffrey Bilhuber; 163 Dominique Kieffer's house in Normandy; 164 Chris Bortugno's house in upstate New York; 165 above left Mr & Mrs Sagbakken's cabin by the sea (Norway), interior design by Helene Forbes-Hennie; 165 above center Axel Vervoodt's house in Belgium; 165 above left Ali Sharland's house in Gloucestershire; 165 center left Julie Prisca's house in Normandy; 165 center Frank Faulkner's house in upstate New York; 165 above right Fritz & Dana Rohn's Connecticut house; 165 below left a mountain retreat in Colorado, designed by Ron Mason; 165 below center Fritz & Dana Rohn's Connecticut house; 165 below right Peter and Marijke de Wit of Domaine d'Heerstaayen in the Netherlands; 166-167 Michael Leva's house in Connecticut; 168 Mrs Fasting's cabin in the Norwegian mountains, interior design by Heiberg Cummings Design; 169 above left Fritz & Dana Rohn's Connecticut house; 169 above center Ali Sharland's house in Gloucestershire; 169 above right Fritz & Dana Rohn's Connecticut house; 169 center left Robert & Josyane Young's house in London; 169 center a house in Virginia designed by Solis Betancourt; 169 center right Robert & Josyane Young's house in London; 169 below left a house in Connecticut designed by Jeffrey Bilhuber; 169 below center a house in Virginia designed by Solis Betancourt; 169 below right a house in Connecticut designed by Jeffrey Bilhuber; 170 above left Chris Bortugno's house in upstate New York; 170 above center Alex van de Walle's apartment in Brussels; 170 above right a cabin in Aspen, designed by Holly Lueders; 170 below left Axel Vervoodt's house in Belgium; 170 below center a house in Virginia designed by Solis Betancourt; 170 below right James Gager & Richard Ferretti's Pennsylvanian house; 171 Chris Bortugno's house in upstate New York; 172 Peter and Marijke de Wit of Domaine d'Heerstaayen in the Netherlands; 173 left Julie Prisca's house in Normandy; 173 right Axel Vervoodt's house in Belgium; 174 Dominique Kieffer's house in Normandy; 175 above Wingate Jackson, Jr and Paul Trantanella's house in upstate New York; 175 below Fritz & Dana Rohn's Connecticut house; 176 above left Agnès Emery's house in Marrakech; 176 above center Dominique Kieffer's house in Normandy; 176 above right Michael Leva's house in Connecticut; 176 below left James Gager & Richard Ferretti's Pennsylvanian house; 176 below center Agnès Emery's house in Marrakech; 176 below right Peter and Marijke de Wit of Domaine d'Heerstaayen in the Netherlands; 177 Alex van de Walle's apartment in Brussels; 178 a cabin in Aspen, designed by Holly Lueders; 179 above left A house in Virginia designed by Solis Betancourt; 179 above right Mrs Fasting's cabin in the mountains, interior design by Heiberg Cummings Design; 179 center left James Gager & Richard Ferretti's Pennsylvanian house; 179 center right a mountain retreat in Colorado, designed by Ron Mason; 179 below left a house in Oxfordshire designed by Todhunter Earle; 179 below right Mrs Fasting's cabin in the Norwegian mountains, interior design by Heiberg Cummings Design; 180 above left Alex van de Walle's apartment in Brussels; 180 above right & below left Ivy Ross & Brian Gill's home in Galisteo; 180 below right Axel Vervoodt's house in Belgium; 181 Ivy Ross & Brian Gill's home in Galisteo; 182 Fritz & Dana Rohn's Connecticut house; 183 above left & right Peter and Marijke de Wit of Domaine d'Heerstaayen in the Netherlands; 183 below left Peter and Marijke de Wit of Domaine d'Heerstaayen in the Netherlands; 183 below right Chris Bortugno's house in upstate New York; 185 Frank Faulkner's house in upstate New York;

author's acknowledgments

There are so many people who are involved in creating a book like this and I want to say an enormous thank you to everyone who allowed us to photograph their wonderful homes. I would also like to thank my friend and publisher Jacqui Small for all our collaborations. I would like to thank Simon Upton for his inspirational photography and for being as enthusiastic as I am for interiors—both historic and modern. My editor Sian Parkhouse and Managing Editor Kate John have been thoroughly professional, understanding, encouraging, and have made even last-minute caption writing fun (almost!). Maggie Town has surpassed even her high standards with the design. Jill Bace has been at her most inspirational contributing to the text. Nadine Bazar found some wonderful locations, as did my dear friends Gloria Stewart and Fayal Greene. Julie Brooke and Mark Hill gave their support as always, and I really could not work on these wonderful projects without the support and understanding of my husband John Wainwright, and my children Cara, Kirsty, and Tom.